WHO AM I? DRUGS TO DREAMS

WHO AM I? DRUGS TO DREAMS

David Harrison

ISBN-13: 9781518628153
ISBN-10: 151862815X
Library of Congress Control Number: 2015917201
CreateSpace Independent Publishing Platform
North Charleston, South Carolina

Dedication

I dedicate this book to all those on a healing journey towards their true identity. My prayer for you is that you will recognize the labels, lies, and scripts that you carry and be restored to a place where you dream and fly into your destiny.

Acknowledgments

Thanks to my wife Ashley, the love of my life and best friend who has sacrificed so much for me to follow my dreams and stood by me the whole way through!

Thanks to my boys Judah and Rowan who inspire me daily to dream.

Mom and Dad, thank you for supporting me through the journey of writing this book. You have graciously allowed me to be vulnerable not just with my story but our story. I love you guys more than words can say.

I want to especially thank my father Scott and my mother-in-law Bobbi for your tireless help of editing. I would also like to thank Chad Block, Faith Hazell, and Nathan Densley for proof reading and feedback.

Thanks to Will and Heather Taylor and Brad and Jan Minton who let me spend time writing tucked away in their cabins.

Thanks to the Create Space team for such amazing job with everything.

Endorsements

"David is a great storyteller and has laid his life bare in all its raw and honest detail for all to see. He tells of his highs and lows, including his incredible journey back to his faith and walk with Christ. It reminds me that God, in his unfailing love, never gives up on us, never holds our past against us, and is always ready with arms wide open to welcome us home. Thanks David, you are an inspiration to all us mere mortals."
Tony Kirwan
President & Founder
Destiny Rescue

"David has taken us on a kingdom journey of transformation. Readers will be inspired as they hear the God story in David's life. He challenges us all to get more healing for our hearts by discovering the goodness of God who created us for something amazing. He reminds that we are brought into our true identity when we get a hold of God's love and affection for us. There is so much hope in David's story that brings us into dreaming and dreaming brings us into changing the world."
Rick Pino
Heart of David Worship Center
Austin, TX

"Dave writes from his heart and his heart is to surrender everything to the Lord Jesus. I appreciate Dave's vulnerability all the way through the book. As he shares his journey through life, he lets us in on the good, the bad and the ugly. I could identify with the journey because I have been on one myself (and I am still on one). Many others reading this book will also identify with Dave's journey to find their lost identity and perhaps be aided in their journeys of discovery.

I believe Dave's struggle to find his personal identity in Jesus Christ will be an inspiration for many young people still on their own passage of discovery. He writes with passion, honesty and vulnerability, which enables others to examine their own hearts in the battle of life to "become" what God created them to be. His encouragement for us to dream and not just set goals will bring faith and hope to everyone who has a desire to find and follow the will of God for their lives."
Graham Bretherick
Registered Psychologist
Author of Healing Life's Hurts

"I believe this world is filled with people who are pursuing a life of wholeness, faith, and health. My dear friend Dave is a leader in this pursuit and in these pages his life is laid out before us - robust with lessons to be learned and applied to our own. The world is busted and broken and filled with people who are the same. Why don't we try something new, something different, something right? Why don't we live full healthy hope-filled lives helping and changing the world as we go? I personally saw Dave change from a broken man to a world changer and I believe the questions and lessons in this book will inspire you to do the same. Let's change the world!"
Nathan Densley
Director of the Martyr's Life Initiative

'Storytelling is the most powerful way to put ideas into the world today.' - Robert McKee

'Stories have power. They delight, enchant, touch, teach, recall, inspire, motivate, challenge. They help us understand. They imprint a picture on our minds. Want to make a point or raise an issue? Tell a story.'
- Janet Litherland

"A good story can often hold a readers attention long enough to reveal life-changing truths. In 'Who Am I – Drugs To Dreams', David Harrison has shared his life journey in a way that allows you to feel both his pain and his exultation. It's no wonder that you finish with an unexpected hope. David is the real deal and his life is proof of the healing power of our good Father. Enjoy!"
Larry Moore
Executive Director – AYMI

"The road of life is riddled with challenges, pain, and struggle. As you travel through the pages of this book, you will be confronted with this reality. You will also discover that, in light of all these difficulties, we have a very Sovereign, gracious God who believes in us, walks with us, and is on our side. What starts as an explanation of Dave Harrison's journey to find himself, ends with a question that we must all come to grips with: Who am I and what will I do with my life?"
Rev. Brian Fuller
President of Eston Bible College

"Proud of Dave's journey captured here in simplicity and authenticity, which will bring hope and create space for belief in the God who rescues and redeems all who are searching."
Sheri McConnell
Director
Youth, Artists and Volunteer Engagement
World Vision Canada

Author's Note:

Some of the names of the people mentioned in this book have been changed. I've done so where I have felt anonymity is important.

Forward

**"I love you, but I'm starting to hate you!
I don't want to hate you, but I can't help it!"**

Those are words no parent ever wants to hear, but that's what Dave's mom and I were being blasted with in one of our most painful moments. The greater tragedy, though, was that David's pain was so much deeper…so much more wrenching….than anything we were experiencing that horrible night in our tiny kitchen.

And there was no fast turn-around. That night David walked out of our lives emotionally and it wouldn't be long before he moved out physically. We watched as he was pulled down a destructive path that would hold him much longer than we would have ever dreamed. There was still much torment to come for Dave, and much loss.

But there was a turn-around. It wasn't a 'single-event' kind of thing. It was a process that David describes in this book, desiring to help others who are trapped in pain and lies about who they are. And who they aren't.

Reading Dave's story hasn't been easy. Reliving hurtful times and things we may choose not to remember can be hard. Things like watching your kids hurt. Things like knowing the choices you made and didn't make as a parent radically affected them. Things like failing to protect Dave and his brother and sister at a critical time in their lives. Revisiting failures as a father was anything but fun. But, thank God, that's not the end of the story. It's not the end of my story, and it's not the end of Dave's story.

This is Dave's story.

And Dave's story isn't just for those who are lost and drowning like he was. It's also for those who just haven't found their way yet. It's for anyone asking, ***"Who Am I?"***

SCOTT HARRISON
A Proud and Happy Dad

Book Synopsis

Who Am I? Drugs to Dreams is an autobiography. It tells the journey of a young man who leaves his old life behind to follow God after the tragic death of a friend. David's search exposes him to many different walks of life as he travels the world in search of deeper purpose and truth. After multiple trips to Thailand, working alongside missionaries reaching out to those trapped in the sex trade, David begins to dream of making a difference. David's dream inspires others as he shares his vision of healing and restoration for those who have been rescued from the sex trade. The writer also shares his own journey of recovery, beginning with his sexual abuse at the age of six, moving through the substance abuse of his teen years, and describing his increasing awareness of his own need for healing and restored identity. It is only when David understands *who he is not* that he can begin to understand *who he is.* David's story will inspire people of all ages to get healing for their hearts and fight for their dreams.

Table of Contents

Introduction

Over the past seven years, I have been on a healing journey, a journey of setting aside labels that were put on me as a young child. When this journey began, I felt broken—broken and unfixable. I wanted to end my life. After a great deal of struggle, I am now writing my story. To get to this point, I have had to acknowledge and reject the negative beliefs and expectations—the negative scripts—that society imposes on us and which we too often impose on ourselves.

The main script I have had to erase from my life is the one that told me I was dumb. I wasn't stupid: I was set up for failure in a school system that was not right for me. But because I did not believe I was intelligent, I limited my own opportunities for the future. Now, after going through college and launching a great career, I have rid myself of that lie and replaced it with my own script: I am brilliant, creative, determined, and a gift to society. *Wow, did I just say that?* By flipping the script of believing I am stupid, I am now able to look at the other lies I have believed about myself.

I believe that we all need healing for our hearts. Nobody can go through life unaffected by our world and its negative vibes. Thankfully, there are enough people having lightbulb moments about themselves now that we have more resources than ever for healing and self-actualization. When we start to peel back the layers of our past, we can see what was supposed to be on the other side of the script. When we find healing, we also find freedom—freedom to dream about the future that God has in store for us.

I want to talk about the process of healing, dreaming, and doing. For me, the distance between a dream and its fruition has depended on two key processes: realizing that I cannot go the distance without getting vulnerable and getting help for my heart, and accepting that there is an in-between season for my dreams (a place I think of as a "wilderness"). This book is for people who have been lied to about who they are and for people who feel like square pegs in round holes.

I invite you to join my journey of healing, identity, and the pursuit of dreams.

Part 1: Drugs or Jesus?

1

Drugs or Jesus?

Dear Twenty-Year-Old Me,

You're going to want to sit down and take your time with this letter. I'm going to tell you some things that I don't want you to miss.

Dave, you're going to have to leave your parents' nest. You will have to carve your own path, and every time you think that you've found a way forward, you can be sure that life will throw you a curveball. It will be lonely and it will be painful, but you have no choice: you have to keep walking. For much of your twenties, you'll feel like a round peg in a square hole. You need to keep moving forward, keeping pushing on, because no one will change the shape of the peg or the hole for you. Don't be afraid to ask questions, and don't be afraid to take advice. At the end of the day, you will have to make your own decisions.

Fish live their lives in water. They don't realize that there is a world beyond the water because the water is all they have experienced. Cultural and social norms are the water we all swim in, if you will, and most of us are comfortable floating along with the stream. Many of your peers will seem quite content to drift with the current. You, on the other hand, will spend most of your time charting your own path. You will leave the water and have your eyes opened to many different cultures. You will find options that you did not know were available to you and that will set you on a search for what it's all about. You will recognize that the social and cultural norms surrounding you are quite relative.

There will be days when you feel like a salmon spending all of your energy swimming upstream. Remember: God is leading you, but you have to do the swimming.

There will be days when you feel you cannot take another step. But you will, and every step you take will move you closer to the desires of your heart. You will not always live in the pain you know now; you will come out glowing and full of life. All I can say is that there are very good things waiting for you.

All of the answers lie in finding your real identity. You will need to start by finding who you are not. You have to identify and recognize the labels you have picked up. But fear not: when you find out who you are, you will know where you need to go. It will take faith. It will require you to take risks. It may look foolish to others, but that is what walking by faith is all about. Remember, no matter how deep the pain on your healing journey, the sun will rise the next morning. Lastly, remember that you are not just doing this for yourself but for many. So keep going.

■ ■ ■

As an adolescent, I really didn't know who I was—the question didn't even cross my mind. All my basic needs were met; I was just another fish in the stream. I had no idea that the quest for my own identity would be my life's greatest search.

When I think back to my childhood, I don't have a lot of great memories. I was angry from a pretty young age. I had a great family of five, with an older brother Joel and younger sister Kaylah. We had parents who really loved us kids, but I remember thinking how amazing it would be to grow up in what I considered a "normal" family. My dad was the pastor at Living Hope Community Church in the small city of Estevan, Saskatchewan, and my idea of normalcy was impossible for the son of a preacher man. I wanted to play hockey like the rest of the kids I knew, but my parents told me that we couldn't afford it—and that there were too many games on Sundays.

My desire to fit in began as soon as I started school. From the age of four, I was—unwillingly—a student at Living Hope Christian Academy (LHCA). Not only had my dad planted a church when I was one, but three years later he opened a private Christian school. Every morning, I had to put on my uniform and go to school—with my siblings and parents, and in the same building where we met for church week after week. I was stuck in that little building on Perkins Road six days a week. I felt like I was suffocating.

Being with my family all the time was hard for me, but the awareness of being different was worse. LHCA was a small school, and there were only a few kids my age there. When I met kids from around our block, I was ashamed of going to a church school and sometimes lied about it because I did not want to be rejected. As time went on, I began to hate the church and school. I began acting out at a young age, stealing and getting into fights. In my effort to gain their acceptance, I was willing to do whatever I thought the other kids would like.

My dad was very focused and driven as he pursued the things God had called him to. But I felt like I was just along for the ride, and I wished I could get off at the next stop. In grade nine, I used the Bible against my dad. I brought up the scripture from Revelation 3:16 that said that God did not want lukewarm Christians and would spew them out of his mouth: God preferred

5

that we be either hot or cold. I told my dad that whether or not to follow God was my decision, and that if he would not cut me loose from the Christian school, he was choosing the school over me. My hate for that school was driving me mad, and I told him that I did not want it to drive a deeper wedge between us and ruin our relationship. I told him I was prepared to run away and not look back if he would not let me go—that the outcome of our relationship rested with him. After nine long years of school, Dad finally agreed to let me make my exit.

Even at my most rebellious, I truly loved my dad and knew that he loved me. I just did not want anything to do with his church or school. I was very sincere in my threat about leaving home, and I had already done the classic twenty-four-hour run-away a few times, so it was getting real. I am so grateful that my dad's love for me trumped his "responsibility" for me. He chose our relationship over his anxieties about my leaving the school or his fear of being viewed as a pastor who did not have a handle on his own kid.

I smoked weed for the first time at thirteen and used marijuana and alcohol regularly by fifteen. By the time I turned sixteen, I was getting high every day. We usually took it pretty easy during the week, limiting ourselves to weed, but when the weekend rolled around, it was time to party hard—cocaine, magic mushrooms, and my drug of choice, ecstasy. Although I was relieved to be released from LHCA at last, I was still not happy. I was still an angry teen rebelling against my parents and my religious upbringing. I did not care about anything or anyone outside of my group of friends. I was the black sheep of the family.

As a teen, my brother stayed the way of the straight and narrow. He was in my parent's private Christian school until he graduated and then moved away to university. We did not spend a lot of time together as adolescents, as I was off hanging out with the party crowd while he was hanging out with his friends from church (although most of the time you could find him out fishing). I always liked my brother and looked up to him, but we lived very different lives and did not have much to connect on.

My sister was four years younger than me. Unfortunately, I was a mean brother to her. I knew she looked up to me for all the wrong reasons. I was popular and known for being a wild guy. I was mean to her because I did not want her to look up to me and follow the path I had chosen. I was being protective of her in a way that was hurtful. I alienated myself from my family as a teen, spending as little time at home as possible, out with my friends living in the fast lane.

In 2003, at the age of nineteen, I graduated from high school (two years late). I moved out of my parents' home into an apartment with a couple of buddies so I could drink and smoke as much dope as I wanted in the comfort of my own home. I had not been a part of my dad's church since the age of fourteen. I loved my family but wanted nothing to do with Christianity—which was everything to them.

My purpose in life was simple: getting high, getting drunk, and hooking up with girls. A perfect weekday evening for me entailed large amounts of weed, poker or Mario Kart, and getting munchies with the boys. We were a close-knit group of friends who shared everything with one another. I had emotionally abandoned my family and was content to share my life with my friends. I was going nowhere fast, and I didn't really care.

All that changed without warning one cold, fall day in Estevan. I was fueling up my truck when an acquaintance told me that my friend Dana had drowned the night before. His body had not been recovered, but other friends who were partying with Dana saw him fall through the ice and not come back up.

Dana and I had played club soccer together for ten years. I could not believe he was gone. I had never really thought of death before, and definitely not about death taking someone at the age

7

of twenty—especially someone who was my friend. I went into shock. I knew I had to go find my dad. I needed to talk to someone who had a grasp on life and death. When I found him at the church and told him what had happened, Dad grabbed me with his great big arms and shoulders, and wrapped himself around me. He received me that day with such warmth and comfort.

In all my years of rebellion, I never doubted that God was real, and I never truly lost my desire to follow Him. When I was thirteen, I was radically baptized in the Holy Spirit at a youth retreat in Melfort, Saskatchewan. I remember walking out of that service and staring into the star-filled sky as an awareness of the greatness of God filled my mind and soul. That evening, I thought my life would look different when I headed back to Estevan, but the feeling of awe was short-lived. My anger was just too strong. Anger made it too hard for me to follow the Lord's ways in the church, and I chose not to think about that night again.

I now had to think about the reality of God and what it all meant. I needed some answers. I did not do much talking with my dad that day. I just wept. I wept because my short life had flashed before my eyes. I wept because I realized that I had known of a great treasure, but in my selfish rebellion I had never shared God with my friends. I felt responsible for what I suddenly saw as severe neglect, and a great weight came upon me. I had not been a witness for God when I knew that He was real. Suddenly, nothing else in my life seemed to matter.

I felt that if I did not change my life and live for God, I would be letting my friends believe it was OK for them not to know Jesus as their Savior. I believed everything I had heard about God, and it terrified me. I had come from a loving Christian home and had had an encounter with God. None of my friends had had either of these opportunities. As much as I wanted to avoid the reality of my friend Dana's death, I could not. In a panic, I moved out of the apartment and went back home.

I told my dad that I was looking for a way out of the life I was living but didn't know how to turn it all around. He had planned to take a three-week trip to the Philippines to do some preaching and help a ministry called Frontline—headed by Dad's friend Jeff Pessina and his Filipino wife, Rowenna—construct a church building. He thought it might be good for me to go with him and get away for a bit. I agreed and booked my tickets.

Only days before we left, I spent a night taking ecstasy and smoking dope, and had a bad trip that lasted for three days. As the darkness drew near each night, I was unable to leave my room. If I did not die from the experience, I was seriously considering taking my own life. I knew the trip was nearing, but I could not even leave my bedroom—let alone leave the country. But by the grace of God, I arrived in the Philippines.

The city of San Pablo, and Frontline Ministries, were unlike anything I had ever seen before. The people seemed so happy and full of life. Every night they had an open-air tent meeting in whatever part of the city they felt God had told them to go. They were bringing God and the church to the people. It was something I had never seen before, and I was pretty overwhelmed by the whole experience. As great as it was to be there, I still had no peace: there was a fight going on for my life. I shared a room with my dad and another Canadian pastor, and they told me that I kept them awake every night screaming and shouting curses. The battle raged within me even as I slept.

My deliverance into a walk with Christ did not come from an anointed speaker, or a salvation altar call, but from a young boy of maybe ten or twelve. Every night at the tent meetings, a couple of young lads came to sit by me and joke around. They taught me little magic tricks, and we had some good laughs. During my last week there, just before the service started, one boy asked me why I never went behind the stage to pray with the other Christians. When he asked me that question, time stood still. The spirit of

God was resting on this child, and I could see Christ in his eyes. I didn't know what to say—that I was still trying to figure out how the Christian thing worked for me? That I was not ready to give up my friendships and addictions? No, there was nothing I could say to this boy. I stood up without saying a word, walked behind the stage, gave my dad a little smile, bowed my head, and began to pray. This would be the beginning of a wild journey with Jesus.

I wish I could say that I went home, never touched drugs again, and led all of my friends to Jesus, but this was not the case. I remember calling up a couple of buddies when I got home—I wanted to get together and say good-bye to an old friend, Mary Jane (marijuana). I had a romantic relationship with Mary Jane: she and I had been through a lot, and we were inseparable. She came to all of my soccer games, and she was always with me at school. Pretty much everywhere I went, there was Mary Jane. I remember telling my dad I was going out to have one final puff. He was upset, but I thought he just didn't understand.

In reality, of course, it was I who did not understand. After going out for one last hoorah, it was a good month before I touched the stuff again. I was doing my best not to be in places where substances would be present. But weed and other substances had a strong hold on my life, and it was harder to lay it all down than I had thought. I never seemed to make it for more than about a month before I would say, "Oh, maybe just one last time." And I would say it again and again.

I had been back from the Philippines for a good six months when I went to a party one night. I was not drinking alcohol, because I knew I would not be able to control myself. I remember a buddy calling me into his car. A whole lot of smoke and temptation was waiting for me there. As I settled in, I realized they were smoking not just weed but Coco-Puffs (weed and cocaine in a joint). I had not seen cocaine for a while, and I fell victim to her luring pull. I was confused and defeated.

I had to admit to myself that I had addiction issues and that even if I had never become a Christian I was in a place where I would need help. My friends and I were not kids anymore, and we found ourselves getting in over our heads with trouble when we were partying.

Looking back now, I can see that when I drank I would get out of control. I would often find myself in the middle of trouble, whether it involved fighting, dealing drugs, or theft. Thankfully, I didn't spend more than sleepovers in jail in the drunk tank, but some of my friends did time in prison for things like burning down the house of a rival drug dealer or assault causing bodily harm, and at one point even assaulting a police officer. For some, prison was not the worst result. Death was.

Estevan was a rough town. The excessive partying took the lives of too many of my friends and people I went to school with. I knew nine people—all of whom I went to school with and partied with—who died within a few years of finishing high school. Some died from violence or suicide. Most died from drinking and driving. Two guys I knew played chicken on motorbikes. Neither pulled away and both died. I look back and can't help but think, not only about the possibility that I could very well not be here today, but also how all of the people I know who died *should* be here today. I can count up to seventeen people I went to school with who died in a city of ten thousand people over the past ten years.

Each time I heard of another death I would be heartbroken for the families and friends of the lost ones and feel so upset at the lives that were ending far too soon. With each loss I felt a little more traumatized by the harsh realities of life and death, but it pushed me harder to find a more meaningful, healthy, and purposeful life for myself and my loved ones. I knew there was a better way. I would give myself to pointing in the direction to life away from death. I knew the answer would be found in God.

A week after my relapse, I was sitting on a tire tube at work having a smoke and feeling sorry for myself, and I asked God what I was supposed to do. I had no Christian friends, and I knew I did not have the power to stay away from drugs. I heard the Lord tell me, clear as a bell, to move to Calgary, Alberta. I went home and told my dad what I had heard, and then phoned up my brother, still a passionate follower of Christ. My brother, who lived in Regina, Saskatchewan, called me later that day and said he had talked to his friend in Calgary: I could move in with him. Two weeks later, I loaded up my truck and moved to Calgary.

Walking away from my friends was the hardest thing I had ever had to do. They were more than just friends: they were my family. I felt like I was abandoning them, and I felt incredibly alone. But I knew that I could not stay with them and remain sober. I was now a disciple of Christ. So if I was going to leave everything for Christ, to follow and serve Him, where would I go? It only made sense to try and get back to the place that had touched and changed my heart in the first place—*to the nations.*

When I was in the Philippines, I had met a group of Canadian young adults from a mission called Lifeforce—a mission my brother had been a part of for a couple years. Lifeforce is much like a better-known ministry called Youth with a Mission (YWAM). Young adults spend a few months in classes at the base and then go on a mission for four months. The base for Lifeforce was in Calgary, which is why I felt God was telling me to move there. I would work until Lifeforce began, saving as much money as I could. I needed to get back to that special place across the ocean where I had felt God so strongly.

I ended up working in concrete construction with a group of guys who were Lifeforcers. My construction foreman, Ben Wiebe, remembered me as a kid in Bible camp back in Saskatchewan. One day at work, he reminded me that he had been my camp counselor and that we had soaked his bed in vinegar. I told him that I had a selective memory and could not recall that, although the five-kilometer run we had been punished with first thing the next morning was coming back to me! It turned out that I would be joining Ben and his wife Sarah's Lifeforce team and that we would be going to Zimbabwe, Africa.

2

Trouble in the Jungle

Discipleship training at Lifeforce was called boot camp. Guest speakers, men and women of God, came daily to teach us. They shared their own testimonies, describing the ways they had seen God move in their lives. I was a sponge, taking in as much as I could. As I listened to all their amazing stories of the miracles God had performed in their midst, my childlike faith was growing. I was blessed to have great teachers expanding my knowledge of God. One teacher in particular, Sheri McConnell, spent a lot of time with me and took me under her wing.

Sheri quickly became a friend and mentor. She was very down to earth, and I never felt like I had to fake anything around her. I always felt like there was an unspoken pressure to be better than I thought I was when I was around other Christians, but I didn't feel that way around Sheri. Sheri was passionate about social justice, a great teacher who inspired me with sobering stories and statistics that opened my eyes to the injustices going on in our world. I am thankful for the insight Sheri gave me at the beginning of my Christian walk, as social justice would become ever more important to me on my journey. After three months of training, I was itching to go to the nations and preach the Gospel.

Our team of seven was ready to go and share the Gospel in Africa. Zimbabwe was experiencing political unrest at the time, so we were told to avoid all conversations about politics. When we saw soldiers and government officials, we were to look straight ahead. I remember smelling smells I had never smelled before, tasting food I had never eaten, and best of all, meeting wonderful people in a culture I had never experienced. Going to schools and churches surrounded by the beautiful people of Zimbabwe was amazing. As I continued with my Bible study and prayer, I was blown away by the wonders of God and the kingdom. I was walking in a season of discovery, seeking the riches of God.

The greatest thing happened to me when I was in Africa: I read the Gospels for the first time. In all my years as a pastor's son, I had never read one of the Gospels cover to cover—although, to be fair, I don't know that I ever read *any* book in its entirety while I was growing up. When I read about the life of Christ, I felt simultaneously amazed and foolish (foolish because it took me so long to read the full story of Jesus, which was the foundation of the Christian faith).

I was pleased and surprised to discover that Jesus was actually a radical kind of guy—someone who went against the grain of society. What really amazed me was Jesus's encounters with the church of his day. The Jewish leaders had issues with Jesus exercising the authority that God the Father had given Him. Religion wanted to tell Jesus what to do and where to go, but Jesus was not having any of it. It made me think of my experience with Christianity. I had felt stifled by Christian school and its rules: no hair past the collar, no earrings, school uniforms were mandatory. The idea that I had to look a certain way to win God's approval had always seemed seriously out of whack.

I was having a eureka moment. During all those years I had been mad at God and Christians, it was the spirit of religion that I really should have rebelled against. Growing up, I had seen Christianity as a set of rules to follow, and these rules became my reflection of God. Until I read the Gospels through for the first time, I never had anything concrete to put my faith in. I wondered how many other people in the world were making the mistake of analyzing the church and all of her flaws, and then projecting the imperfections of the church into a flawed image of God. It was that day that I realized the religion that I thought I hated so much was the very thing that held me back. I was the one who was religious attempting to live a life based on Christian ideas and principles until my recognition of the life of Christ. I was living my life by the letter and not by the Spirit. Any thought of God and the Christian life apart from a firm understanding of the incarnate God Jesus Christ, living and dying for the forgiveness of sin, for all humanity, was just that…an empty religion.

My time in Africa would not be easy. It had many high points, but halfway through the mission, I wanted to go home. I had gone to Africa with false expectations that I would have an experience similar to my time in the Philippines. Unfortunately, I did not see eye to eye with everyone on my team—and they definitely did not see eye to eye with me. I was still quite rough around the edges, and I was very upset about what I saw as the unecessary activities I was supposed to take part in. I particularly disliked the idea that I had gone all the way across the world to act out scenes in dramas. I felt like we were mere Christian entertainers instead of Christians doing the things I was reading about in the Bible like seeing miracles and healing the sick.

Of course, I knew what I was getting into: during our time in boot camp, we had learned several dramas to perform in churches and schools. Having to act in them brought me back to painful memories of Christian-school plays I'd done as a kid. The funny thing is, I was a good actor; I just didn't like doing all of the practicing or performing. Acting out dramas was OK for a while, but after a few months, I was getting very sick of it. As I read the book of Acts, I read about amazing miracles performed by people filled with the Holy Spirit. I had not traveled to another continent to be an entertainer. I wanted to see God move in power. Unfortunately, in my lack of maturity, I started to think I was alone in my desire for a radical mission.

About halfway into the mission, I got what I was asking for. I went with my leaders to a church that had a strong message of deliverance—casting demons out of people and breaking curses. The pastor was a tall and broad man, who spoke with passion about delivering people from evil spirits. At the end of the meeting, there was an altar call for people who were having bad dreams and being attacked in their minds. I noticed something very interesting. It was only women who came forward for prayer, and there were only men on the prayer team. As the men started praying for the women, they began to shout at them. It turned ugly fast, with the men actually pushing the women around as they prayed for them and commanded evil spirits to come out of them. It was horrific to watch the obvious abuse taking place.

I was in absolute shock as I watched the injustice of men abusing their power and perverting the Gospel. We just sat by and watched as the abuse continued. I went home stunned that day both because of what I had witnessed and because I had not done anything about it. It bothered me that I had no idea of what I could have done even if I was brave enough. A few weeks later, I got the news that the church that was hosting us wanted us to go spend a week with the "deliverance" church on an outreach mission in the jungle. I found out later that the pastor of our hosting church had only just met the pastor of the abusive church and had no idea of the dangerous situation he was sending us into.

I remember asking my team leader what he would do if they started pushing the women around again and his admitting that he wasn't sure. That was fair enough, because I had no idea how to handle it either. My leader, Ben, had come from a very conservative Mennonite background. He told me that he had never seen a demonic manifestation before and that we would have to take it one day at a time. The next thing I knew, we were heading off into the jungle with the pastor and his all-male team.

The pastor took a liking to me as we spent our first day together, and I actually started liking him, too. As we walked through the hillside to witness to the more isolated people, I started to feel comfortable around the pastor and came right out and asked him why he and his team were pushing the women as they prayed at their service. He simply replied that there was no pushing: the spirits themselves were moving the women around. All I could come up for a rebuttal to his answer was, "Oh, I see." The week was actually going pretty well, and I started to think— naively—that maybe the "prayer push circle" was just a one-time thing.

It was the last night of our time out in the jungle. The air was thick, and the spiritual atmosphere was intense. At the end of the pastor's final sermon, he called people to come forward for prayer like he did back at his church. Only this time he asked me if I would pray with them. I agreed, but as soon as I began pray- ing for the young woman who approached me for healing, one of the young guys put his hand on her head and started to push her around. I grabbed his hand and told him not to touch anyone I was praying for, and then I stopped praying and took a backseat for a moment. Once again, the women came forward for prayer and the men lined up to pray—or more accurately *prey*—over them. As the abusive prayer began, so did the screams of the women. It was horrible to watch, and I was becoming infuriated.

I looked over to our team of seven scared-and-confused white missionaries stuck in the heart of the jungle and wondered what the heck we were doing there. In a moment of youthful naïveté and outrage, I began pushing the men off the girls, telling them to stop what they were doing. I reminded the pastor that he had told me that they did not push people when they prayed, and as the giant of a man towered over me, I could hardly breathe. It was then that the Spirit of God came to him, and he began to cry. I had been calling out to God for a move of the Spirit for hours the night before. I had great compassion for the pastor and saw that he had a misdirected heart but a big one. The meeting came to a halt, and after a moment of stillness and confusion, people went on their way.

I was overwhelmed and unsure what I should have done about the abusive prayer, because no one else was doing anything. My leaders were overwhelmed by my actions. Everyone on the team was upset and unsure of what was going on. I was the only team member who had been at the earlier church service where we saw the initial abuse take place, so the experience was a first for the rest of the team. It was after midnight when we all packed into our van, the guys stone-faced and some of the girls crying. They—quietly, indirectly—accused me of expressing some male bravado, the very thing I thought I had been combating. I was told to have the book of Philippians read before the next night to learn something about humility.

The experience had been very traumatic for me. It was awful to see the abuse of power by the men over the women, and the trauma went deeper as the leaders who had stood by watching the abuse take place passively reprimanded me. I had had many amazing kingdom experiences on our Africa trip and many good laughs with my team. But from that point on, I could not shake off the confusion and hurt of what happened that night in the jungle. After I let my leaders know how upset I was about being passively reprimanded without actually being told what I was in trouble for, I was told we would talk more about the jungle experience, but that didn't happen.

I had never been put in a situation like that before, where I could not clock out at the end of the day. I was in tight quarters, where I could not move freely, for four long months. I understood more about Jesus than ever before, but I could not imagine that I would ever put myself in a situation like that again. More about that later.

A lot of anger had built up in my heart during the last half of our mission. Familiar feelings of rebellion were pushing me further away from my team and leaders. After waiting for months with great anticipation for my mission trip to start, I could not have been happier when it was over. I was overwhelmed with a flood of emotions. I was sad, angry, and disappointed. I felt like a failure. All I wanted to do was to go back to something familiar; I wanted to see my friends.

I contacted some Estevan friends who had moved to Calgary to pick me up at the Calgary Airport upon my arrival in Canada. I could not get away from my team soon enough. I got drunk out of my face that night and had to show up for the next day's debriefing hungover. Anger turned to depression and depression to shame. I had been on a three-day drunken bender and showed up a day late at the beginning of Lifeforce, and now I had gotten drunk within hours of being off the plane from my mission. I was a mess, but I was still focused on knowing more of God. I wanted to move forward with Jesus. In my immaturity and lack of character, I thought it was everyone else who had a problem, that *I* was ready to move on. The comical part was that I had to go back to my old job doing concrete, as I did not have any other options. As mad as I was, I thought God had a pretty good sense of humor: my Africa team leader Ben became my direct foreman, and I went to work with him every day.

Over the years, I continued my relationship with the Africa team leaders. As I write this portion of the book, I want to honor them and say that I love them. I cannot imagine how taxing it would have been to be my team leader! I had so much to work through—it is to their credit that they did not kick me off the team as I worked out my messy salvation in the beginning of my walk. The Wiebes continued taking teams across the world for the next several years, making big waves for the kingdom and loving the hell out of people wherever they went.

After my Africa mission trip, I said I would never do Lifeforce again. The Lord, on the other hand, had different ideas. Another year rolled around, and my brother Joel and his wife Sonja moved to Calgary because they were preparing to take a Lifeforce team to Thailand. I was still feeling pretty bitter about my Lifeforce experience, and I was still not completely free from the persuasions of drugs, alcohol, and girls. About a week before Lifeforce started up again, I had a big slipup. I got drunk again but this time went home with a girl. I was deeply ashamed and I felt horrible. I was feeling quite low when my brother asked me if I would be interested in joining his Thailand team because a couple of kids from his team had dropped out. I knew in my heart that I was supposed to go with them. I was desperate for another God encounter, and I was desperate for freedom from my addictions. I gave notice at my job and signed up. I had no idea what I was getting myself into and how Thailand would change me.

3

Thailand

I had a good relationship with my brother, and that made going back to Lifeforce a lot easier. Most importantly, I would be going back to Southeast Asia. Joel and Sonja had been to Thailand before and had made previous connections for our trip. There were several of us on the team: skateboarders, dancers, and a multimedia guy. Joel and Sonja had become friends with a Thai girl name Angel while in Thailand and flew her to Calgary. Angel was going to play a major role on our team as our interpreter and guide. Angel stayed with us for a few months to help educate and prepare us for our Thai mission, especially for the city of Pattaya. Even with her help, and as adventurous as I was, nothing could prepare me for my Thailand experience.

Pattaya had originally been a small, peaceful fishing village a couple hours south of Bangkok. It became a docking point for American soldiers during the Vietnam War, who gradually transformed that innocent village into what is now: the sex-trade capital of the world. People from all over the world come to escape their mundane lives and become self-appointed kings to be worshipped by Thai women—well, sometimes women. Pattaya is also a major hub for homosexual prostitution. Gay men and boys sell themselves for money there, but the main attraction are the ladyboys. The ladyboys have all been to see the surgeon. Males are made to look like exotic women with big breasts and some go further with their surgeries. Although Angel and Joel had done their best to prepare us, words could never have been enough.

We arrived in Bangkok and continued our trek east to Pattaya, which would be home for the next four months. I often describe Pattaya as a little Las Vegas. The difference is that gambling is not the main attraction: sex is. "Walking Street" is two kilometers long, full of brothels lit up brighter than Christmas trees. I was filled with horror rather than shock at what these beautiful Thai women were doing or anger at the evil men who had put them in this position. I felt horror because I was enjoying having attractive women calling out to me, making me feel desired. I felt horrible because part of me wanted to abandon my mission and join the party. It was only by the grace of God that I was able to fight the temptations that called out to me.

When we talk about brothels and the sex trade in Pattaya, it is easy to imagine what we have all seen in videos made about the sex trade: grim footage of unhappy girls and women being pushed from room to room. But this is not what is seen by the window-shopping tourists. The women who represent the bars appear to be the happiest people on earth. They are given a script to follow to lure men in as they compete for customers with other bars. I only went into a few of the closed-door bars where the "go-go girls" danced. Once you enter the bars, you see more average-looking girls—who look like they are on the edge of a breakdown. Everything on the surface is made to lure you in and steal your soul.

I kept telling myself I was there to help, and I was, but there was a constant fight not to let my soul take pleasure in women constantly calling out to me. The struggle became easier the longer I stayed in Pattaya. Nothing was hidden there. We saw constant abuse take place in broad daylight; it could happen anywhere in the city. The desire I initially felt to join the party faded as I spent time working with its aftermath—the city's numerous orphans and widows.

We worked with a beautiful Canadian couple named Fred and Dianne Fowler. They had started an orphanage, and we were able to spend a lot of time hanging out with the kids and helping with a major renovation project. These wonderful children had had no one to care for them until they found a home at the Mercy Center. To this day, I get a tear in my eye as I remember seeing and feeling Jesus's love for the kids. The Mercy Center was amazing. I just could not spend enough time there.

Other ministries were working with the women who were no longer an asset to the sex industry. Some women are forced to leave sex work when they reach a certain age and no longer appeal to customers. Others leave when they can no longer take the abuse. Their minds shut down, and they become mentally ill. We also worked with ministries that served the ladyboys. One particular ladyboy we got to know was dying from AIDS. My friends Jeremy and Wao Carter had established a drop-in center where ladyboys could rest and experience fellowship in a place where nothing was expected of them. It was both beautiful and humbling.

There are not enough ministries to meet the great need in Pattaya, but the ministries that are there are amazing. Their lights were shining in one of the darkest places on the earth. After seeing the ministries repel the darkness, I reflected on Apostle Peter's message that we should look forward to the day of the Lord but be patient because there are more souls to be saved. This made a lot of sense to me. The people I served in Thailand were caught in the clenches of death—as I once was.

The ministry where we spent the most time was called the Crossing. It was a drop-in center for youth and young adults. It was one large room, open to the street, with ping-pong, video games, musical instruments, and more. The main attraction, however, took place on the street itself. The Thai guys were *kanong* (crazy) about skateboarding. I personally had to come out of five years of skateboarding retirement to get in with the guys. After cracking some bones, I quickly remembered why I had given it up in the first place: I was no good at it!

One way we were able to bless our new friends at the Crossing was by building them a half-pipe and some ramps for skateboarding. That half-pipe became common ground for youth and young adults all over the city, a place where they could come escape the darkness. I built amazing relationships at the Crossing. I was blessed by my new Thai friends' passion for Jesus and felt completely at home with them. The sense of community I experienced there reminded me of my time in the Philippians. People there shared everything and came together often.

I did not come out of that Thailand experience with stories of saving lives or rescuing innocent people from sex slavery. I did come out with a heart bonded to the Thai people and a desire to see their chains of bondage broken. I knew my heart was forever knitted to the cause. I wanted to get back there someday and give my life to them. I felt much better coming home from Lifeforce this time and was really excited to get back and tell people about how we saw God's display of love, power, and grace in us and through us.

A few months before I left for Thailand, I had started going to a new church called Harvest Fellowship. When I got back to Calgary, my pastor asked me to share some of the experiences I had there. I spoke about the brokenness and darkness of Thailand and the need for the Gospel there. I testified about the time our team went to Angel's home village and saw the kingdom of light break through the darkness. We spent the week in schools, spending time with kids and teaching them English. The guys would put on skateboard clinics, and the girls would dance to a multimedia presentation. After a week of presenting in schools, we were asked if we could do our presentation for the whole village. The stage that we were given to present on was unreal. The people of the village lived in extremely humble homes—some of them shanties—but in the middle of the village was an ornate Buddhist temple. It was quite a different stage for us, to say the least. We were amazed as the entire village of around three hundred people showed up. The spiritual atmosphere was very intense as I prayed for the village. After our presentation, we told the people of the village that our God was a God of love and that he wanted to heal them. We invited them for prayer, and four little old ladies (one of them Angel's auntie) came forward.

After a group of our girls prayed for the ladies, Angel's auntie grabbed the microphone and shouted out, in Thai, that her painful knee was healed. She began jumping up and down in excitement, and then everyone rushed forward for prayer. Angel and I prayed for one lady who had lost most of her vision. She had what looked like a sheet of ice over her eyes. As we prayed for her, we watched that grayness lift completely off her eyes until she was able to see again. It was amazing to see the power of the cross breaking into an uncontested part of the world. There was no representation of the church in that village, and I knew that something had started that evening that could not be stopped. Several people came to our door the next day asking us to pray for them and wanting to receive Christ as their Savior.

Back in Canada, there was great excitement that day in the church as I shared my story. I felt well received (which is not always the case when coming back from missions), and I felt like I could keep the passion going in Canada. At Harvest Fellowship, I found my first sense of community living in the "real world." I had made friends with some guys who were fun to hang out with and who were taking their walk with the Lord seriously. It was an amazing season of my life: God was giving me the Christian community I so longed for.

Our church put on a conference, and there was a divine appointment waiting for me in one of the breakout sessions. Its speaker, Keith Hazell, was a prophet and the father of Life Links Church, the family of churches I grew up in. Keith was a very special man whom I remembered coming to speak at our church when I was a little boy. Even at a young age, I got excited when men of God visited my dad's church. I was aware of the anointing they carried. Keith was a regular visitor and a family friend.

In Keith's breakout session, he shared the story of his prophesying and teaching in communist (and not so Christian-friendly) China. China allows Christians to gather only in registered churches administered by the government. Someone at one of Keith's unauthorized gatherings had received word that the police were on their way, and the congregation fled, officers hot on their trail. My hair stood on edge as Keith told us of lying low on a mountainside, hiding from the authorities. They prayed to God, who made it supernaturally dark all around them, and the police walked right by them.

Next, Keith put on a video that blew my mind. The Chinese church Keith was visiting was worshipping in an overcrowded room, led by one energetic man giving it his all on his not-very-well-tuned guitar. As they worshipped, the glory of God fell on them. That glory was not confined to the video. As I sat in that room, I was overwhelmed by waves of God's presence. It looked like the video was going out of focus, getting all blurry. Keith said that the glory cloud had filled the room they were worshipping in, just as it had in 2 Chronicles 5:14 (NIV), "The priests could not continue their service because of the cloud, for the glorious presence of the LORD filled the Temple of God".

I was awestruck. I had never seen anything like this before. Since becoming a believer, I had read story after story of the kingdom of God coming to earth, and signs and wonders following, but I had not seen them taking place in the lives of believers.

I found Keith after the meeting and told him that I was astonished by the video. Keith responded that he had likewise been very excited by my testimony about Thailand a few weeks prior. He told me that he was on his way to Romania in a month to be with a church led by David Norton and his wife Miha. They were young like me, in their midtwenties, and they were seeing a great move of God among the young adults there. And then a shocking thing happened: Keith asked me if I would like to go with him!

4

Signs and Blunders

I was pretty starstruck with Keith, and I was honored that he would ask me to go with him. I wanted to be in Keith's shoes. Nothing would be more amazing to me than traveling the world and ministering. It seemed like an obvious next step to join Keith on his trip and soak up whatever I could from him. I went home that night and told my dad and everyone I could about the opportunity I had been given.

There was only one problem. In order to fly to Romania, I had to go through Germany. Germany was hosting the World Cup that year, and the cheapest round-trip flight I could find was $3,500. I had not been back from Thailand for very long, so not only did I not have money, I was in debt. I was gutted. I e-mailed Keith in despair, telling him I could not accompany him. As far as I was concerned, I had just missed out on one of the greatest opportunities I would ever get to propel myself into a ministry to the nations. I was confused because I was so sure I had felt the Lord give me a green light about going to Romania.

A few months later, Keith contacted me saying that another opportunity had come up to go to Romania. The church in Romania was hosting a young adults' camp and wanted our church to bring a team of musicians and people to join their prayer team. Keith would not be joining us on the trip, which was a bummer, but I felt really good about going. The Lord provided 100 percent of my finances for the trip, with the church generously giving me the finances needed without having asked, and I was on my way.

I had developed some really great relationships in my new church and was pumped to go minister with them. Our church's young adult leader, Corey Stickel, would lead our team. Corey approached me with an e-mail he had received from David Norton in Romania. David wanted to give a heads-up to those who would be joining his wife Miha's prayer team. The letter said that prayer would be marked out for six hours a day and that she had high expectations of our commitment to the team. In short, the letter was to warn/prepare us for her militant style of leadership.

When we arrived and met the Nortons, I did not see Miha as a militant person at all—until, that is, the first morning of prayer. I was late, and she gave me "the eye." I did not shrink down but fell into line. I also meant business and was not frightened but encouraged by her serious attitude toward the souls we were praying for. I learned the power of speaking in tongues from Miha. We would stir our spirits by speaking in tongues for a minimum of a half hour before joining together in corporate prayer. There were two of us from Canada and five locals of Romania. As we prayed in the spirit, Miha said that my prayers in English often mirrored what someone had just prayed in Romanian. There was a strong sense of the prophetic as we interceded for the unbelievers at the camp.

After the first day, it seemed like momentum was really picking up in terms of spirit. I was not aware of this, but David's father, Bill Norton, had prophesied that there would be awesome signs and wonders during the camp. Gold dust settled on us as we prayed: at one point, as we prayed in the forest, the glittering whirlwind swirling over our heads made me think of *The Chronicles of Narnia*. Another time, as we prayed in a circle, I saw a vision of a fruit cracking in half. I had never seen a fruit like this before: it looked like a cross between a pineapple and a jackfruit. An amazing fragrance suddenly filled the room. One girl said it smelled like a rose, but I knew it was a fruit from heaven. The amazing thing was that you could smell the fragrance only inside the prayer circle.

On the last evening of the camp, as we were worshipping, I felt the Holy Spirit tell me to take some video to take back to our church for presentation. I had to leave the service and run across a field to go get my camera from my room. When I got back to the service and began recording, I could not believe my eyes. The screen on my camera was blurry, kind of like Keith's video from China. As I held onto the camera, I knew I was holding something very special. I captured about a five-minute video of a glory cloud filling and sweeping through the room.

I showed everyone the video after the service, and one guy who had received salvation and the baptism of the Holy Spirit that night said he had run out of the service to wash his face because he could see the glory cloud the whole time and thought he was going blind. In both instances—in China and Romania—there were a few people who could see the cloud, but most were oblivious to what was taking place until they saw it on the video. I was extremely excited. Little did I know that this excitement would send me into one of the darkest seasons of my life.

I hoped the video might open doors for me in ministry, but when I shared that thought with Corey, he looked at me with concern and said that we should never use God's glory to further our own goals. I was cut by his words and felt misunderstood. I remembered Keith saying that others had asked for his video of the glory cloud in China but that he did not feel it was an appropriate thing to pass around. I went from cloud nine to cloud one pretty fast, but nonetheless, I knew I had something pretty special in my possession. How could Keith and Corey not understand that being invited into churches to show the amazing signs and wonders of God was a way to bring glory to Him and to raise the faith of the church?

I was about to learn some very hard lessons about humility, about not going where God was not leading me, and about God's value of character over gifting. It was never about the signs and wonders but about the sacrifice and prayer that went out for the young men and women of the camp. When we got back to Calgary, I felt a covering of grace and favor lift off me. Although my local church was excited about what had taken place in Romania, that was not the feeling I got from others. I put blame on others for how I felt as I testified about the impact of our prayer and about the signs and wonders that followed. I chalked my audience's apparent lack of enthusiasm up to what I saw as the faithlessness of the Canadian church. I went from disappointment to anger, and then to alienation. I know now that they were not faithless but rather saw a young man who had a long journey of character-building ahead of him. I did not yet have the character to carry the calling God had marked out for me. I needed to learn some big lessons before he would bless my testimony again.

I had gone from one of the best years of my life to one of my darkest moments. I felt like I was losing everyone and everything. I severely injured my back while falling with a wheelbarrow full of concrete and lost my job, and I felt my most cherished friendships dwindling away. I began having suicidal thoughts, and I was very afraid that I was going to act on them. I was terrified for myself and for my family. I was dealing with depression at a level I had never experienced before, and I knew that I needed to ask for help before things got worse. I told my parents and my pastors what I was going through, and my pastors referred me to a Christian counselor.

5

The Black Dog

My counselor, Dr. Randy Johnson, was a very nice guy. He welcomed me into his office and began a series of questions to see what was causing all the heartache. I told him of my struggles, of how I had hurt my back and was not able to do construction work anymore. I told him that I'd had amazing experiences in Thailand and Romania but that I did not know how to make the transition back to ordinary life. Dr. Johnson gave me homework: he said he wanted me to put together a fifteen-year life plan. I should identify what I ultimately wanted to do with my life and map out the steps to get there. He assured me that what I was going through was very common for people my age.

When most people think about a fifteen-year plan, they think about their careers. I had worked in construction for three years and could not do it anymore, but I was not upset about that. I had never been any good at construction anyway. Part of my depression, in fact, came from feeling that I was not really good at *anything*. It made me feel like I didn't have much of a chance at a successful future. Most people in their twenties feel at least some sense of security as they work toward a career and a sustainable future. As I thought about how much I sucked at everything from mechanics to construction, I began to feel more panicked than ever. I had felt stupid from a very young age, and I was insecure. I had assumed that I could make some kind of a living working with my hands, as long as it was not too technical. But now my injury made that impossible. What was I going to do? I was at a complete loss as I sat in that counselor's chair.

After going home and giving it some thought, I put pen to paper. The only place where life seemed to make sense to me was overseas in the mission field. My heart was in Southeast Asia. I dreamed of being a missionary to Thailand one day. I phoned my dad and talked to him about what it might take to make my dream come true. He said the only real way he had seen it work was for missionaries to be sent from a church they were part of. So after giving it some thought, I decided it was time to move back to Estevan and put in some years of service at my dad's church. I thought that the counselor had done an exceptional job after all: I now had a direction for my life that seemed to momentarily lift the heavy cloud over my head.

When I got to Estevan, I got a job that was amazing for me. I worked for the city at the ice rink. What good Canadian does not love the thought of driving a Zamboni for a living? It was straightforward work that was easy on my body, and the pay was good. I was feeling relieved, as things seemed to be turning around. I had a job that was not going to strain my back, and I was ready to serve the church until it was my time to sail away.

At that time, I had one Christian friend in Estevan, Nathan Densley. Nathan and I grew up in the Christian school and church together. We had seasons of being close as kids, but it never stuck for too long, as I wanted to go down the wrong path and Nathan did not. When I gave my life to the Lord in the Philippines, Nathan was there on a Lifeforce team. It was good to reconnect, but I did not know that the Lord would bring us to a very close relationship in the future. Thankfully, Nathan was in Estevan at the same time as I was, taking a break from Lifeforce. It made a world of difference to have a Christian friend there with me.

After a few months in Estevan, I unexpectedly got an invitation from Keith Hazell to come to Lethbridge, Alberta, for a conference called "Under the Radar." The conference was to be a gathering of prophets, and I was ecstatic to get an invitation. I asked Nathan to come along with me, and the trip was the kickstart to a renewed and powerful relationship. He was great company as we drove along the frozen highway, listening to music and praying. One thing Nathan and I had in common was a passion for prayer. We could pray and prophesy together into the late hours of the night.

The conference was small and intimate, with a lot of my childhood heroes and some new faces all packed into one room. I looked at Nathan and thought, *What the heck are a couple of schmucks like us doing here?* It was amazing to be around the high level of anointing in that place as the powerful worship, prayer, and prophecy went forth. Romania was still fresh in my mind—as a wonderful testimony, but also as a fleshly wound. I was aware of the pride I felt at being invited to this conference, and I cried out to God for mercy and humility. I had learned my lesson.

I could never thank Keith Hazell enough for inviting me into his circle of trust after my dramatic departure from Calgary after our Romania trip. Keith sometimes freaked me out with his prophetic gifts. He always seemed to have a handle on what was going on with me without needing to have a conversation about it. It was his mercy and care for me that picked me up above what others might see as someone who was not a good fit for the ministry. Keith was not really impressed by "cookie cutter" Christians. He understood wild guys like me, guys who needed some time and grooming but were full of potential. It was encouraging as a young man to feel honored and trusted among the giants of the faith. Nathan and I headed back to Estevan with our cups filled.

Shortly after our return, Nathan called me over to his place to give me some news: he was leaving Estevan for the United

States, where he would be attending a prayer movement with a guy named Lou Engle. Nathan, my only close Christian friend in Estevan, was taking off to North Carolina. I hated the thought of being without him. I was sad, and I was also a little concerned about Nathan taking off, as I knew it meant I would feel lonely and have to be more careful about who I hung out with.

Things actually went pretty well for a while. I had learned from past experience that I would not be able to resist substances, and I knew I needed to lay low. I had a couple of my old buddies around to play sports or watch movies with, and I was a junior youth leader in my dad's church. My social life was kind of minimal, and working with youth was not really my forte, but it was a place to serve. All in all, it was not too bad. I was living at home, saving up some cash, and waiting for my day to come. Then, several months after moving back to Estevan, everything took a turn for the worse.

It was summertime, and I was still working for the city, doing some landscaping in the city parks. One day, as I was cleaning up at the cemetery, I realized that I was working beside two of my friends' graves. I felt a heavy wave of emotion come over me. I was overwhelmed with deep sorrow and a sense of loss. A voice filled my mind, asking me why I desired so strongly to be a missionary across the world when my friends were dying here in Estevan.

I was once again reminded that I had never felt settled or accepted as a Christian. I felt like I did not belong in the church or with my old group of friends. I reluctantly agreed with that voice as I felt grief and anger rise up within me. I thought maybe I was wasting my time, that I would never be good enough for the church or the life of a missionary. I had no desire to walk away from God, but when I made an agreement with that lie, I made up my mind to walk away from the church and give my life to my old friends in Estevan.

I went straight to my dad's office from work and told him I was going to be taking a break from the church, that my friends needed me. He pleaded with me and said that I was heading back down the road to death. But my mind was made up, and I moved out of my parents' house within hours and moved in with an old buddy of mine. Although I knew not being a part of the church would cost me something, I felt the sacrifice was worth it. I did not see any point trying to fit in while living life in the context of the church. After all, I was quite different than its members.

It did not take long to feel weighed down after leaving what little Christian community I had. I gave up on my sobriety and started drinking a little more every day. I got to a point where I would polish off a bottle of wine with supper and then drink a six-pack after that. I was getting drunk every night and heading to work hungover every day. Over the next two months, I got a good look at what my life would have been like if I had not finally turned my heart to God. I became an extremely angry person. My day consisted of waking up, going to work without eating breakfast, forcing myself to eat a small lunch despite my hang-over, and going home to have supper and get drunk again. My anger was my source of energy. I used it to get myself through a day of work. My coworkers saw a drastic change in the person who had been telling them about how Jesus had changed his life. I started smoking pot again and basically gave up. I lost a lot of weight fast and looked like a different person. I was so angry and so ashamed.

One night while lying in my bed trying to sleep drunk and stoned, I had a demonic manifestation of a snake in my bed. I was terrified. I knew the reality of the spiritual realm and called out to God for help. It was two in the morning, and I knew what I had to do. I picked up the phone and called my dad.

Once again, I was on the phone asking for help. I quit my job that morning, telling my boss that I had substance-abuse issues

I needed to deal with. I went over to my parents' house as a broken young man, once again feeling the weight of failure. Eight months prior, I had moved back to Estevan to serve and eventually be sent out from the church as a missionary. Now, sitting with my dad in the basement of their house, I wept. I cried from a deep place, confessing that I knew I had to move away and never come back. The thought of not even being able to live in the same city as my family was both devastating and debilitating. At that point, I was not worried about my prior aspirations to become a missionary. I just knew that I had to get away.

A few months earlier, I had received an invitation to take Keith Hazell's granddaughter, Tiffa Hazell, to her high school graduation. Some months before my crash, I had connected with her father, Jeremy, at the "Under the Radar" conference in Lethbridge and had agreed to go spend time with the Hazells in Lethbridge. I had not known what I would go through shortly after saying yes.

I had written Jeremy and his wife Faith a month into my fall and told them that I was not doing well and was not fit to take their daughter to graduation. Faith started writing me daily, encouraging me in the Lord. I honestly did not know how to handle her kind words during that time, but when I knew I had to get the heck out of Estevan, it only made sense that I pack up my belongings and see what Lethbridge had to offer.

I was once again heading down the highway with all my belongings. My vehicles kept getting worse and worse, and my belongings less and less. This time around I was cruising in my classic Lincoln Continental. There was brokenness in my soul but a glimmer of hope in my heart. I knew this had to be—and would be—the last time I went down that dark road. I vowed to never touch drugs again, no matter how heavy the pain of my heart. I had been snared in the enemy's drug trap for the last time.

When I arrived, I could see that the Hazells really wanted to take care of me. They did not seem to feel that I needed to confess or be fixed but rather that I needed to be loved and cared for. They made sure I was there for supper every evening and welcomed me into their family without expectation. I was not made well overnight, by any means. Winston Churchill, one of the finest leaders of our time, struggled with depression and referred to it as the "Black Dog." Churchill described life with the Black Dog as a world with no color. I could relate: depression was always with me, and I could not function throughout the day. I remembered my time with my counselor in Calgary and felt slightly embittered because I had failed to carry out the plan we had devised at our meetings.

Shortly into my stay with the Hazells, Jeremy said something to me that I had never heard from anyone else in the church: "Maybe you should see a doctor." With Jeremy's help, I made an appointment and was given medication for depression and anxiety. After a few weeks, I was able to stay on an even keel throughout my day—something I had never experienced before, or at least not from what I could remember.

This stability came at a price. One of my coping mechanisms prior to the medication was descriptive writing. Now I started to take my brokenness and write about it in pictorial allegory. It was strange, but the writing I had come to rely on seemed to be gone. I felt a bit sad, as I had found a good chunk of my identity in my writing. Where the writing was before, now there was numbness. It was like taking Advil for a headache, where the Advil masks the pain, but the disturbance causing it is still taking place. The trade-off was being able to get a job and get through the day without feeling like I wanted to die. I started working for a dry-wall company. I managed the company's equipment and jumped in with the laborers where I was needed. I was feeling for the first time in a long time that I was going to be OK.

During my stay with the family, I had been reading about baptism and the idea of dying to myself. I was challenged by the words of the Apostle Paul, who said in Galatians 2:2 (NIV), "My old self has been crucified with Christ and I no longer live, but Christ in me. The life I now live I live in the body, I live in the Son of God, who loved me and gave himself for me". I wanted to learn how to lay down my fleshly desires and give my self to a life of being led by the Spirit. After leaving Estevan this last time and going through hell, I knew I needed to let go. I talked to Jeremy about my desire to be baptized and come out of the waters a new man, leaving my past in the past. I was sick of having one foot in the grave due to my love for and a false commitment to my friends. I was ready to admit that I could not save them and that the best, most loving thing I could do for them was to live my life completely for Christ and let them watch me burn from afar. My commitment to a life surrendered to Christ would start with the waters of baptism.

Jeremy and his family had planted a church in Lethbridge called Mosaic Christian Fellowship. Being part of a church plant was exciting. I was baptized by Jeremy and the Mosaic crew down at the Old Man River in Lethbridge. It was such a relief to be baptized and to believe that something supernatural was taking place. I made the decision not to look back. As we stood in the water, Jeremy preached about the new names the apostles received after their spiritual rebirths—Simon becoming Peter, and Saul becoming Paul—which spoke of Christ giving us a new spiritual identity. Hoping for a prophetic answer as we were walking back to our cars, I asked Jeremy with a big smile what my new name was. He only smiled back at me—although a bit prophetically.

Later that evening, my mother phoned me to tell me that she had a word from the Lord for me. She went on to talk about Jesus renaming the disciples, offering the same message that Jeremy had shared in the water. And then my mom said that Jesus had renamed me "Accepted."

I had not felt accepted for most of my life. I did not realize at the time just how empowering that word was for me. Jesus saw me as accepted; He wanted me to see myself as accepted. I had felt too low and broken to feel real acceptance most of my life, especially in my early Christian years. I was dealing with rejection, which crippled many of my relationships with friends, family, and churches. I was relieved to have that prophetic declaration made over me, and I was eager to begin the journey of believing it.

Part 2: Who Am I?

6

Truth Life Documentary

Shortly after laying down my friends to the Lord, the most beautiful thing happened. Two of my close friends in Estevan gave their lives to Jesus. I received a phone call from a long-time friend, Alex Johnson, who was living in Vancouver. Alex was going through a hard time. He was dealing with depression like I had been, wondering if he was losing his mind. Looking for a way out of the depression, he had turned to spiritualists who prescribed a mantra to chant, which did not help. I told Alex he should leave Vancouver and come spend some time with me in Lethbridge. The answer was easy: he needed Jesus. I put Alex in a position where he could experience the presence of Jesus and could not escape! I took Alex with me to Life Links Bible camp in Montana for three days of worship, prayer, and teaching.

One morning after waking up in our tent, I was talking to Alex about how real God and His kingdom on earth truly were. I used *The Matrix* to illustrate my point. In the movie, after Morpheus explains that the Matrix is all around us but that it must be experienced to be believed, Neo is left with a decision. Morpheus says, "You take the blue pill, the story ends; you wake up in your bed and believe whatever you want to. You take the red pill, you stay in Wonderland and I show you how deep the rabbit hole goes."

I told Alex that God was offering him a way out of his pain and confusion. If he believed and gave his life to God, he would have to give him everything and life would never be the same. Later that day, as we were sitting in a meeting, the preacher relayed the same message. What happened next blew Alex away. The speaker played the exact clip from *The Matrix* that we had been talking about that morning. I knew the Lord was pursuing Alex, calling him, and now Alex knew, too.

Shortly after that visit, Alex decided he needed to leave Vancouver and move to Lethbridge to stay with me for a while. I was overwhelmed with joy that the Lord was answering my prayers. My friends were coming to Christ after I had laid them down. Alex was a very gifted guy, and God's call was obvious in his life early on. As far back as I could remember, Alex always had a video camera in his hand, filming us as we skated or got into mischief in good old Estevan. After high school, Alex pursued his passion for film in postsecondary education. With Alex's talents and my travel experience, we decided to pool our creativity together and make a documentary.

There was one missing link. Alex and I had a friend named Dustin Ross, who had yet to come into the picture. Alex and Dustin were always running around with a camera making videos when we were growing up. When Dustin found out that we were taking steps toward doing some filming overseas, he was very interested. Dustin was in his last year of a Sociology degree at the University of Saskatchewan, and he felt the buzzing energy of the adventure we were about to embark on. He needed to know more.

Alex and I had plans to be at a Life Links Church conference in Medicine Hat, and we asked Dustin to rendezvous with us there. It was a perfect opportunity to get Dustin in a place where we could talk about our plans for film while immersed in the presence of God. He may have been set up—just a little—but he took the bait. He could see that what was happening among us was very real. After a few late-night talks, Dustin wasted no time in giving his life to Christ. He dropped out of school to join what would be known as TruthLifeDocumentary.

The skies were the limit. We were all living on faith, with not much in our wallets, but there was no one richer. We were inexperienced businessmen and visionaries, but the creative energy we were feeling every day was too much to ignore. We felt that walking into the unknown was worth the risk. Not only were two of my Estevan friends now as hungry for God as I was, but the Lord wanted to use us! I was about to embark on what would be some of the most exciting months of my life.

The Lord was doing deep work in my heart and was about to give me a new and different set of challenges. There was nothing normal or average about the season I was walking in. I had a kingdom on earth mentality every day. I was reading a book called *Rees Howells Intercessor*, by Norman Grubbs, that would challenge and stretch me in ways I did not know were possible. Rees Howells was an intercessor—a man of prayer—from Wales, whom the Lord had used in extraordinary ways. Mr. Howels had lived through World War Two and served as a missionary in Africa. He had an extreme personality, and I recognized that he must have sacrificed a lot to be as fruitful as he was.

After reading *Rees Howells Intercessor*, I prayed that the Lord would use me like he had used Howells. I felt the Lord tell me that there were some things that he wanted me to lay down. First, He told me that I needed to give my car away; second, He told me that I was not to shave (just like Howells in the book); and lastly, I was to give all of my brand-name clothing away. I had the reaction you might expect from someone hearing something like this: I wondered if I had really heard God. It took me no time at all to understand that I had.

I phoned my brother Joel and told him that I would like to give him my car. My brother laughed and replied that he and Sonja had prayed the evening before that the Lord would supply them with a car. Next, I stopped shaving. I looked pretty ridiculous—I could not grow a beard—but I was humble and obedient. Then it was time for the clothes. Let me say that surrendering the clothes to the Lord was far harder for me than giving away my car or not shaving. Ever since I was a little kid, I was well aware of social status and desperate for acceptance. Wearing nice clothes had always been important to me. Now I packed all my brand-name clothes into a couple of garbage bags, where they sat in the corner of my bedroom for a few weeks. The clothes revealed a lot about my heart. After much wrestling, I packed the bags up and gave them to my friend to give to a needy family. This personal season had brought me amazing freedom and fruit. Having my heart close with the Lord and having two of my best buddies on a journey with me was more than I could have asked for.

TruthLifeDocumentary was turning from dream to reality. We were taking our ideas and putting them to work. We went to Estevan, filming pieces of our own story along with interviews of friends, family, and our old favorite school teachers. We were extremely interested in identity and life choices, asking why people went down the roads they did. I think some people thought we were crazy, but others were able to connect with the creative energy and got excited. I was dealing with skepticism toward the apparent social structures of life. I, for one, did not want to be a part of what I saw as a societal trap: get a loan to go to school, get married, get a house and a mortgage. I did not believe that I needed to be a part of a debt cycle that would not allow me the freedom of choice or the ability to pick up and go on a whim. We had other questions about addictions and about why people never left their hometowns. We wanted to know what made people tick.

We wanted to grow our filming business and experience. The next logical step was to go overseas and do some filming. I suggested that we go film in Thailand, working with my friends who were serving people caught up in the sex trade. I recalled that the time between conceiving the idea and booking our flights was only a few hours. We were on a serious high: I was pretty sure we were going to be filming the next *Invisible Children*.

We packed up all our gear and headed over the big blue divide to a place I knew all too well. We spent the majority of our time in Pattaya, the sex playground of the world. It has been said that Thailand has the biggest smile and the biggest broken heart. This was nowhere more obvious than in Pattaya. I was very familiar with Walking Street, but Alex and Dustin were awestruck as they saw the bars and brothels lined up for miles. We did not make it more than five steps down Walking Street before a beautiful Thai woman asked us to join her for a drink. I had warned Alex and Dustin that the ladyboys were aggressive, but they were still surprised when they jumped on us, requesting piggyback rides that quickly turned into games of bucking bronco. It did not take long for the guys to see that Pattaya was a playground for the wild and broken.

While walking in Pattaya near a place that was a hub for gay clients, I saw something that totally rocked me. A thin gray-haired Caucasian man who appeared to be in his late sixties was unashamedly fondling a seemingly emotionless teenage boy who was working the strip right in the middle of the street in broad daylight. As I looked at the man I curled up on the inside. All I could see was pure evil. Part of me wanted to run away as I was so sick by the shameless darkness I was encountering, and the other part wanted to knock the old man out and tell the kid to run. But I knew this was not how you fight the darkness—fight the sex trade. For now our weapons were our camera and our determination to expose the sex trade to a world of people who would join our cause of fighting sex trafficking.

We were filming all the sights and sounds of Walking Street when we met Sunny. Sunny was a beautiful girl from Bangkok, and she agreed to do an interview if we would come into her bar for a drink. Sunny received money for every customer she could lure in off the street with her beauty and charm. We asked Sunny the most obvious question: why was she working on Walking Street? She had good English and the obvious ability to be doing something else. She gave an answer that we would hear over and over. She had been pressured by her family to make money and to send a chunk home. She became emotional when she talked about the little brother she had left in Bangkok. It was apparent that she was desperate to make more money in order to protect her brother from going down a similar path.

I asked Sunny what her dream job was, and the answer hit me like a ton of bricks. Sunny wanted to own and operate a flower shop. It was not an outlandish dream. She was not asking to be an astronaut or a multimillionaire—she wanted to run a flower shop. I felt my heart shrivel up. I wanted to get Sunny off the street that night. I wanted to see her dream job become a reality. After we left Sunny, I looked at every bar girl differently, and my heart hurt for them a little more. I wanted to see every one of them set free from abuse.

Not only were the girls giving away their bodies and their dignity, but being a working girl in Pattaya was extremely dangerous. Drunken men with a lust for power and dominance towered over these vulnerable girls. Many of these men were career criminals and horribly violent people. They exercised power over their victims and took it to unimaginable levels. I remember seeing a man with a giant swastika tattooed on the back of his head pulling a terrified girl through a McDonald's and feeling sick and helpless as I watched.

I could spend only a limited amount of time on Walking Street. The evil in that demonic playground zapped my energy to the point that I got physically sick. I would retreat to my room and evaluate what I was doing there, what I was doing with my life. Time seemed to stand still as I considered my own identity and the broken selfhood of the Thai people I was witnessing once again. One night I had a burst of creative energy. I took apart a box and made a little cardboard sign that said, "Who Am I?" We took that sign all over, getting photos and film clips for our documentary as random people held the sign and told us a bit about themselves. For me, the "Who Am I?" sign became an inspiration. The photos of kids, women, and ladyboys holding the sign as they worked on Walking Street—whether they were selling fruit, flowers, or themselves—were powerful images. It felt like we were holding on to something powerful, yet we felt so powerless. We wanted nothing more than to tell the people we interviewed that this evening would be the last they had to work on Walking Street, but we couldn't. We had no solution.

Thankfully, we also got to spend time with people who were making a real change in the lives of the broken. My friends, the Carter family, lived in Pattaya. Jeremy and Wao were such a good connection for me. Jeremy, who was from England, married Wao, who was Thai, and they had two beautiful boys, Jordan and Jonah. They were caring people who loved the lowest of the low. Jeremy did an interview for us and said, "As they go through the sex trade, people lose their place due to age, looks, insanity, and especially sickness—AIDS is prevalent. When they are no longer useful to their employers, they live on the streets and will sell themselves for a plate of food." Jeremy and Wao gave themselves to these who were at the bottom of the ladder. They worked with broken people where they were at. It was a good place to debrief and see the hope, love, and acceptance that was there was for the brokenhearted.

Jeremy helped me understand one thing about the brokenness of the Thai people that could be easily overlooked. It was not only foreigners acting out in their sexual brokenness: many

Thai men patronized the brothels. There were brothels where no foreigner could be found for a hundred miles. The brothels were set up for the local men of the community. Jeremy knew of a father in a nearby village who was training his own children in sexual maneuvers. The man had daughters at the age of twelve, eight, and six, and their services were available for the men in that community.

We had captured some powerful and enlightening interviews and images on film. We had traveled through the bowels of hell and been lifted up on heaven's wings of hope. I knew my life would never be the same. I had hoped to make a film that would inspire change and challenge people to dream and not to be boxed in by social norms. I also wanted to inspire others to get involved in bringing an end to slavery. I wanted to have someone watch Sunny's story and say that he or she would be the one to step in and help make her dream of a flower shop a reality. We had a mission to take the experiences that we had been filming nationally and internationally over the past several months and create a weapon for social justice.

7

Scales

My first memory after arriving back in Canada was going to meet a girl for coffee. Her name was Ashley Scales. Ashley was the prettiest girl around and had the most intriguing charisma about her. We had kindred hearts when it came to the things of the Lord. Ashley was a worship leader, and I loved worshipping and praying together in our young adult group. Ashley and I met at the mall for coffee during the last week of Christmas shopping, and I was absolutely rocked by culture shock. As I watched people rushing around, stressed out as they tried to finish their Christmas lists, I felt a sense of horror, like nothing was real. For most people living in North America, Christmas shopping meant everything, but none of it mattered to me. By the time I met up with Ashley, she had to ask me what was wrong: I was white as a ghost. I tried to explain the world I had just left, but it was all too much for her to understand.

Ashley and I spent a lot more time together over the next few months, and I developed a definite crush on her. Ashley came from a good, successful family. She was gorgeous, funny, and caring. She was an anointed worship leader, and she was too good for me—or at least that's what I thought. One day, as I was cooking my supper, I heard the voice of the Lord—as clear as a bell—tell me to package up my food and start a fast. I did just that. I went down to my bedroom, locked myself away, and began to pray.

I had my iPod on shuffle when all of a sudden, miraculously, a song cut out halfway through and a Graham Cooke sermon took over. Graham was sharing a story from a movie about two brothers and how they differed when it came to girls. One brother was shy with girls and never went on any dates; the other brother was confident, smooth, and quite popular. One day, feeling insecure and jealous of his brother's success with women, the less confident brother told him that he had seen him in school talking to a girl—and that the girl had laughed and made fun of him as he walked away. The brother replied to him that he knew that the girl had made fun of him, but it did not matter. The brother was not afraid of being unsuccessful and said liking her had nothing to do with himself. He had wanted to let her know how amazing he thought she was, and he had nothing to lose in letting her know.

When I heard this message, I knew exactly why I had been called to be alone with God. He had a message for me about my insecurity. I wanted nothing in the world more than to be with Ashley Scales as more than a friend; I secretly hoped that she would put on some weight so I would stand more of a chance to be with her. I knew what I had to do: I needed to be courageous and tell her how special she was—and not give an evaluation of myself while doing it.

I have to admit that it was easier said than done. After all, I was the guy who'd made an agreement with the Lord not to shave: I was looking pretty rough by then. I did not own a vehicle, and I was unemployed. Nonetheless, I got up the courage to phone her late one evening and told her that I would like to come see her. At her invitation, I borrowed a friend's car and drove to her parents' house. I remember sitting silently at the kitchen table as she made us a cup of tea. She was stunning, and I was sweating. It felt like it took hours for that water to boil. She finally sat down and gave me a look that said, "Tell me what I already know you are going to tell me." Still, I had to get it out: "Ashley, I know I don't have a lot going for me right now, but I have to tell you that I think you're amazing. And I want you to know that I mean that as more than a friend."

She was very graceful as she listened to me blabber. I asked her if she would allow me to take her out on a date, and she said yes! I could not believe it—it had worked! Who knew how far a little confidence could go. We did go on a date, but one was just not enough for me. I asked Ashley on another, and her reply freaked me right out. Ashley informed me that after her past relationship had ended, she'd told her dad that she wanted him to be part of the decision process when she began another relationship. In short, I needed to ask for her dad's blessing to pursue her before she would give me another date. As much as I hated hearing that at the time, her character was the very reason I liked her. Ashley's desire to do things right, even if it seemed a bit strange to me, was very attractive.

I arranged to meet Ashley's dad, Doug, for coffee at Tim Hortons on an icy February day. I, of course, had to borrow a car again. Ashley's dad was not an intimidating man, but my current résumé for courtship didn't give me a lot of confidence. Doug was a man of God, however, and after I explained why I was unemployed and looked so scruffy, he did not reject me. Instead, he encouraged me on my journey with God and gave me his blessing.

Ashley and I began a relationship, and I was walking on cloud nine, dating a girl who—in my opinion, and I think the opinion of most of our peers—was way out of my league. I was still focused on developing TruthLifeDocumentary, and my heart for Thailand was still there, but I was just a wee bit distracted.

Alex and Dustin, meanwhile, had been spending their time in Regina, Saskatchewan, connecting with other filmmakers and editing the documentary. I was of no use when it came to the computer editing part of the gig. All of us, Alex in particular, were feeling the pressure that was building: we had put a year of our lives into writing and filming, and all of our resources had run dry. There was a sense that the film needed to be finished pronto so we could move on to other ventures. Alex basically turned off his phone and disappeared into the wind for a month, leaving Dustin and me wondering what the end result would be.

One day I received a phone call from Dustin saying it was done. He was a nervous wreck, and it seemed like for him the film had become more of a curse than a blessing. He mailed me a copy, and as I watched it, I was moved. I personally thought there was room for storyboard improvement, but the bones of the message—this great recognition of how we are influenced by family, culture, life experience, and social norms—were there. The only problem was that the form our message took only really made sense to Alex, Dustin, and me, because it was *our* journey of asking questions.

When we showed other people the film, it was obvious that they thought it was cool but they did not really understand it. After all, it was a film about coming to an understanding of our own lives. It was us saying: *this life does not make sense*. It was likely that an audience that was detached from our journey would not be able to understand it or appreciate it for what it was. I wanted to give the film one last chance. After all, we had poured thousands of dollars and countless hours of work into this project—not to mention that it was never supposed to be about us, but about the people we were supposed to be helping. It was about our friends back home, stuck in addiction and hopelessness. It was about people like us who were looking for answers leading to purpose. It was about the Thai people who needed our help.

We set a date for a public viewing and decided that the best way to make sense of things was to play the documentary and add footage of Alex, Dustin, and me giving short speeches between different sections of the film. I represented Truth; Dustin, Life;

and Alex, Documentary. It would be the communication of our commonalities, our differences, and our questions that could save the documentary. As people begin to fill the auditorium we had rented for the release party, we all felt sick to our stomachs, anxious for the response we would receive. There was some validity for our hesitancy that day: some of my fears came true as I looked at the audience after the film. After it ended, they looked back at me not completely sure about everything they had just seen. It was a big blow to the gut. Needless to say, there was no more editing done. It was what it was.

I was genuinely proud of Alex, Dustin, and myself for everything we had done. I was disappointed that we were not able to come together in the end to produce a product that we were all satisfied with, but it was evident that we needed to take a break. Alex and Dustin went their own way and continued with TruthLifeDocumentary. Their next big opportunity involved being hired by the University of Saskatchewan to do a film based on the recovery from the genocide in Rwanda.

My separation from TruthLifeDocumentary was like a painful death. I had invested so much of my heart and dreams into building TLD, and now the guys were going a different direction. I had to let TLD go and cheer it on from a distance. I knew my next venture would be to get Miss Ashley Scales to fall in love with me and start a future together. As madly in love with Ashley as I was, I could not help but wonder if I was a sellout. I started to think about the message I had been spouting off about not wanting to be "tied down" by social norms and being ready to go on an adventure at the drop of a hat. I had to believe that I could eventually sway Ashley to my way of thinking and that we could live in Thailand one day and together be a part of bringing healing to that country.

As Ashley and I got closer, she got to know more about me—good and bad. I had talked to Ashley about some of my journey toward understanding myself. I told her how I had come out of a dark place and was still working out a lot of pain and uncertainty. I had been dealing with depression for much of my life, and it seemed like much of my search for purpose had been connected to that depression. I told her that I was on medication for depression and anxiety, which may have scared her a bit at first. I also told her that I had been to a counselor when I lived in Calgary and that he had explained to me how common it was for people in their twenties to search for meaning and direction in their lives. I wanted her to understand that I was not alone in the struggle.

Ashley told me that she was very close to a counselor in Lethbridge and that she herself had gone for counseling to deal with past hurts. It was nice to know that I was not the only one who was sometimes in need of help. Ashley told me that her counselor had taught her about repressed anger being a source of depression and suggested that I make an appointment to see if I could get some further help to free myself.

I was so thankful to be surrounded by people who cared for me and wanted to see me get help. My pastor Jeremy had taken me to a doctor, which was something no one had recommended before. And even though I wanted to be on medication for as short a time as possible—it was expensive, and I felt a bit insecure about it—I was grateful. Both Jeremy and Ashley's family thought that the medication was a good thing for the time being but recommended getting counseling to deal with all the bottled-up pain and anger on the inside.

Graham Bretherick, a Christian counselor and a registered psychologist, was a longtime family friend of the Scales family. He had a reputation for helping people deal with anger and forgiveness. He had an exercise he did with clients who were dealing with anger. I was to note anyone who had hurt me in the past or present and do the exercise with each one of these people.

Then I was to write an anger letter to each individual on my list and give the homework to Graham. He suggested that my parents would need to be included in the exercise. Even though I loved my parents, I knew I needed to work through my anger toward them to forgive them.

Graham said not to pull any punches. The letters were not ever to be sent to the person they were written to: their purpose was simply to help me see where my anger *was*. It was a challenging exercise. I was not sure who I was going to be writing to or what I was going to be writing about. Surprisingly to me, forming the letter did not take any time at all. I went home and started writing about my anger. The letter was addressed to my parents. I wrote to them about my school experience, and my anger started to boil over as memories popped up. The letter brought me an amazing awareness of feelings I had not thought about for years.

I remembered my first day of school. I would love to say that I was excited, but that was not the case. I remembered sitting on my parents' couch as Dad explained that my school was going to be at the same place we went to church. I remembered instantly feeling sad and confused. Then I remembered pulling up to the church and knowing it was no joke. My stomach felt sick, which would be a proper foretelling of the next nine years of my schooling life.

The school that my dad started used the Accelerated Christian Education (or ACE) curriculum. There were, on average, twenty kids going to school there, ranging from kindergarten to grade twelve. We all sat at a long desk that hinged on the wall, cut up into little cubicles by slide-in dividers. It was kind of like a life sentence of indoor suspension. The workbooks (called *paces*) had lessons organized from grade one all the way up to grade twelve. It was a good system for kids who were strong, independent learners. Students would start each pace by reading the instructions and then doing the work. If you were like me (where you read the instructions and it meant nothing), you would need to put up a little Saskatchewan flag on your desk to signal that you needed assistance. I was in the same little building on Perkins Street for school and church with my parents and siblings six days a week. I can honestly say that I did not like a single season of life in that school, which I believe was the spark to an anger-filled childhood.

A big problem for a young boy like me who was not an independent learner was in the area of scoring (marking) my own work. After a student would do three or four pages in one of their paces, they would need to go up to a table in the middle of the room and find the matching workbook in the filing cabinet, which was the score key. I had a lot of anxiety about marking my own work. It was often wrong, and I could not bear the thought of going back into the vicious anxiety circle of having to figure it all out again, so I would just mark it as right. At the end of the workbook, the teacher would take us to a separate table to complete a test. If the student failed, the teacher would check the workbook for corrections to see if he or she had been marking it properly or cheating. There were also random checks, when teachers would grab students' paces and score keys to see if they were marking their work correctly. I was labeled a cheater at a very early age.

Once a student was busted for cheating, he or she was given what was called a moral violation. This meant that the student would not be able to go on the end-of-the-month field trip and would receive detention—which, in turn, meant no recess or lunch break. And lastly, the parent of the disgraced child would have to come in to administer a spanking. Luckily for my parents, they did not have to drive down to deliver my spanking. They simply escorted me down the hall as I kicked and screamed all the way to my dad's office.

All of our actions were balanced on a reward-and-punishment scale. If you wore your full uniform—tie, sweater, collared shirt, and blue dress pants (girls having the option of a skirt)—you would earn the right to bring junk food for lunch on Friday. If you did something wrong, you would get a demerit; if you did something right, you would get a merit. I only remember getting demerits and moral violations. I felt like a dumb cheater. I felt like I was all alone in my struggle for an education. The pain of my school years at LHCA would seep into the rest of my school life. By the time I was thirteen, my anger and hurt had led me to marijuana and alcohol. My anger took me down a slippery slope.

Writing my anger letter brought on all kinds of emotion. I felt anger, sadness, regret…and relief. It was relieving to have some understanding about a source of anger in my life. I boiled it all down to being angry at my parents, who I felt were naive to believe it was OK to keep me in their school all those years with no sign of success. I was in my early twenties at the time, so the thought of spending half of my life in that school was unbelievable to me. I knew I was on the track to self-discovery, and I was hopeful. I handed my letter to Graham and was ready to see where he would take things next.

Graham read my letter and told me that I was holding back anger. He said I should rewrite it and not hold back any swearing or cursing. He assured me that I needed to feel released from protecting the feelings of the people I wrote about, as they would never see the letter. I needed to let it all out. It is amazing how we can make excuses for people. There has never been a time that I did not love my parents or know their love. I did feel insecure at times, but I know that was out of my brokenness. Yet the pain was real, my depression was real, and I needed to know that my parents made mistakes and that it was OK to let that anger out.

I never read that letter to my parents, nor would I have wanted to. I was, however, able to talk to them about the whole process.

I sought forgiveness for my anger against them and received a deep-hearted apology for the bad decisions they had made. I would revisit the memories of my schooling and childhood later, as my time with Graham was not an overnight fix. But it was a healing time for me—a time of self-discovery. I understood my journey much more clearly.

8

Redemption

After injuring my back numerous times, I was told by my chiropractor that I would never be able to do physical labor again. I had originally injured my back in 2006, working in concrete construction, and I seemed to reinjure it every six months or so. The last time I was simply bending over while plastic-wrapping a crate at the mustard seed plant where I worked. It was my second and last day on that job. My chiropractor told me that I had the back of an old man and that every time I reinjured myself, it would only get worse.

I phoned one of my Lethbridge buddies to see if I could come try my hand at something completely different than I had ever done before—sales. I became an employee of Bell Canada. It was a steep learning curve, which at first I was actually a little excited about. It did not take long to figure out that I was not a salesman: I repeatedly found myself talking people out of sales to go for a cheaper phone. After finding myself at a loss in the employment ring once again, I became very depressed.

Ashley's mom, Bobbi, asked me what I would like to do if money were not an issue. I thought to myself, *Oh no, not that question again*. In all honesty, my answer had never changed. The only thing that made me feel alive was working with people from other cultures as a missionary. But being a missionary does not pay the bills, and to be honest, I knew I was nowhere near ready for that kind of call in my life. Bobbi asked me if I had ever thought of going to school. I smirked at her and said that I would never get in: my high school grades were less than outstanding. On the inside, I was laughing at the thought of my going to school—*yeah, right!*

It was not long, however, before Bobbi came back to me with a brochure for the Lethbridge College corrections program. It included a list of jobs, from prison guards to probation officers to various community working positions, that I would be qualified for if I completed the program. The jobs actually seemed pretty cool, and the thought of making money doing something that helped people and was not physical labor seemed amazing. I quickly tried to tamp down my excitement, as the feeling of letdown was all too familiar to me.

Bobbi told me that I was smart and that she knew I could do it if I tried. She was a math teacher at the college, and she asked me if I would like for her to talk to the head of the program to see what it would take to get in. I could not help but get excited. Bobbi did talk to the head of the program, who told her that he could get me in without even seeing my high school transcripts. I was doomed—I had no excuse not to try! I decided I did not have anything else to lose and would take a chance at college.

I remember my first week of classes. I was terrified. I was joining a class that had already taken a full semester together. My first real memory of my college career was a psychology course comprised of students from various programs. The teacher went around the room asking what everyone wanted to do for a career at the end of school. I felt myself begin to sweat—everyone seemed so sure of their future direction. I vaguely remembered something interesting from the program brochure and said, "Uuuuhhhh, I think I will be a data analyzer," which was followed by a question as to what kind of data. I just decided it would be best to say, "I don't know," and let everyone else in the class in on my little secret: I was dumb. I thought to myself, *What in the world am I doing here?* and began to hear that little voice in my head say that it was only a matter of time until the bottom fell out of this, too.

After being in school for a few more weeks, I had an astounding revelation. I had enrolled in the corrections program thinking that "corrections" was just a term used in social work, much like the corrections I used to get at Christian school. I found out that the Department of Corrections was actually a government agency that worked with criminals. I had a good laugh as I realized that I was the only one in class who did not even realize what he had signed up for! I thought I was in a generalized social work program. As time went on and I settled into my new role as a student, I was actually slowly beginning to enjoy myself.

My girlfriend—soon to be fiancée—and her mom were amazing encouragers. They were also hard-nosed helpers who would not let me off the hook. Bobbi would mark every one of my papers, sitting down with me to go through all of my mistakes and making sure I understood what changes needed to be made. I was forced to deal with my old archenemy, the comma. After learning little lines like, "When in doubt, leave it out," I actually started to get the hang of things. After all, this was the first time since I was a teen that I had been in school and not on drugs. I was midway through my first year when I began letting go of some of the lies I'd been telling myself.

The greatest lie was that I was stupid. Never in a million years did I ever think I would get into a postsecondary program, let alone succeed in one. The majority of my marks were in the nineties. It was incredible. When I came home to Ashley and Bobbi with marks from my papers and exams, I was usually grinning from ear to ear. It was a lot of work, but it was paying off. I could not believe it.

I literally could not believe it, and that was when I had a eureka moment. I was almost a year into my two-year diploma program, pulling off terrific marks but still feeling like I was going to fail. It all seemed too good to be true. I thought that the truth would come out soon enough, that I would soon wake up from my dream of success in school. The "stupid" identity came from such a place of anger, but it was so hard to get rid of. And yet not only did I continue to excel in school, but I finished the two-year program within a year and a half, graduating with the classmates who had started a semester before me. I was so proud of myself. I was shocked and saw that it was a new day. I still had a ways to go and was fearful of heading out into the career world, but I now had a confidence that I had never had before.

My time at LHCA had woven a lie into the fabric of my identity, telling me I was stupid. It imprisoned me, told me how to live my life. I owed my newfound freedom to Bobbi. It was Bobbi who forcefully encouraged me and did not believe me when I told her of my lack of abilities, who guided me into a place of restoration.

In the summer of my final semester of college, I married the girl of my dreams. A few months before getting married, Ashley and I bought our first home. Ashley worked at her nursing job while I finished school and completed renovations on our new place. Marriage was a new, exciting adventure, and it brought massive change. Only two years prior, the most important part of my life message had been about not falling into the social norms of school, then marriage, then mortgage debt. I found myself starting to feel like a bit of a sellout and was worried that I was cutting myself off from my dreams of one day living in Thailand. I often talked to Ashley about my passion and knew that in order for her to fall in love with the Thai people as I had, I would have to take her there and let her experience it firsthand.

I realized that I had to shelve these aspirations for a while, because I had enough figuring out to do as a newlywed. I was an extremely independent person and had only ever had to take care of myself. Ashley was on the exact opposite end of the spectrum, an extremely dependent person who had always been taken care of. I was doing my own laundry by twelve, making my own lunches for school as long as I could remember, and it was normal for my siblings and me to make our own suppers a couple nights of the week. I worked at least twenty hours a week throughout high school and bought everything on my own dollar. Ashley, on the other hand, had her laundry done for her until she got married and got her first full-time job at twenty-four years old. She had left home for one year to go to Christ for the Nations in Dallas, where she shared an apartment with another girl. Other than that year (not working and in a Bible school), moving in with me was her first time being out on her own.

I remember the moment when I first realized that life was going to be quite different now, as I was no longer only taking care of myself. One morning I walked out of the kitchen with a couple of pieces of toast and casually sat down beside Ashley to eat them. She was very upset that I had not offered to make her breakfast as well. Growing up in my family, we all got our own food, then joined one another for supper—on the nights we even ate together. In contrast, Ashley's parents would never make themselves food without offering some to the other. It was then that I realized that Ashley and I had not just married each other, but we had married each other's families and all the prior experiences that came with them. It was a lot easier not to worry about my fears of missing the boat when it came to my career when I was so preoccupied with figuring out married life.

Both Ashley and I are strong-willed people. We had a lot of different ideas about family life, church life, and life in general. We had to walk through a lot of the fantasy of what we thought marriage was and begin to form our own family culture.

Ashley and I divided our time between work, hanging out with friends, and church. At that point, we were a part of the

Mosaic Christian Fellowship Church leadership team with the Hazells. We enjoyed spending time with people of all ages and spent a lot of additional time hanging out with the young adults in Mosaic. There was a small group of us who were hungry for God and eager to see Him move.

We often talked, prayed, and worshipped late into the night. As Ashley and I got more into the flow of marriage, I felt more room to start dreaming again. It was not hard to dream when I was with my good friend 'Dinkster', who was always on fire for the Lord. We had enjoyed having Nathan Densley with us in Lethbridge for a while at that point. There was also another friend I had made in Lethbridge, Stephen Fulton, who had fallen in love with Thailand on YWAM a few years prior and wanted to go back. I thought it was about time to pray and talk about taking a team over to Thailand. We were surrounded by passionate young adults like ourselves, so I knew it would be easy to assemble a team.

9

Destiny Rescue

I finished my two years of school and knew that the best time to take a trip would be before I got locked into a job. I put together a team of young adults, friends from Mosaic who wanted to come with me and Ashley to do a short-term mission trip to Thailand. Pattaya was the obvious place to go, as that is where all my contacts were, but when our team got together in prayer, we had a strong sense that the Lord was calling us to go into the northeast region of Thailand, to Chiang Rai. I sensed that the Lord was sending us to spy out the land, like in the book of Joshua. I didn't have any contacts in Chiang Rai, so I did some research online and found Destiny Rescue. When I read about the organization and its founder, Tony Kirwan, I knew that this was the place we were to go. Little did I know that Tony would become one of my heroes. Let me tell you some of Tony Kirwan and the Destiny Rescue's story.

While in Cambodia in the late nineties, Tony saw kids in the dump with open sores, swollen bellies, and little or no clothing. Moved by what he saw, Tony poured his heart out to God and sensed an overwhelming urge to do something. He said he remembered praying, "God have mercy on these children," but before he could even get the words out, he felt what he really should be praying was, "God have mercy on me if I don't do something to help these kids."

Tony's young family answered the call, moved to Thailand, and volunteered with a mission organization. Tony heard a story about a Christian man who was offered sex with children for $400. It was after hearing this story that Tony knew he had to do something and developed the vision for Destiny Rescue. They are now an internationally recognized Christian nonprofit organization motivated by rescuing children enslaved in the sex trafficking industry. They are currently operating in Thailand, Laos, Cambodia, Philippines, India and the Dominican Republic. Since 2011, they have saved over fourteen hundred children from sexual exploitation, placing the children in safe houses. They also take care of hundreds of "at-risk" children, often siblings of the rescued, in their Prevention Homes.

After children are rescued, Destiny Rescue empowers them with what they need to recover from their traumatic experiences. The children are provided medical help, counseling, schooling, vocational training and all daily needs in order to integrate back into society. Destiny Rescue works hard to create a loving environment where the children feel valued and have an opportunity to be a kid again.

The information I found online was enough for me to know I had found the right place to go. I got in contact with Tony Kirwan and set up a time for us to come and volunteer and see where our hearts would lead us. I was getting very excited and nervous about taking Ashley with me to Thailand. I was putting all of my eggs in one basket, hoping that she would fall in love with the country that meant so much to me. I knew her heart was amazing and that her heart was for the Lord, which made it a lot easier.

Our team boarded the plane and set out to start our adventure. We began with the yearly Pattaya Praise event, in which worship teams come to Thailand from all over the world to lift up praise and worship over the city. We were a part of Pattaya

Praise our first week there, worshipping the Lord in unity all over the city. Ashley joined a band made up of my Thai friends, and it was so exciting to see her getting connected. A small mob of Christians flooded Walking Street and praised the Lord as we marched from end to end along the brothels, asking that the throne of God be established there. We had a good week in Pattaya, but I was really eager to get to Chiang Rai and see what the Lord had for us there.

Unfortunately, an issue arose for Ashley after we left Pattaya and our air-conditioned motel. When we arrived in Chiang Rai, we were put up on the third story of a house that had no AC. Ashley did not do well with the heat and was getting frantic. She was not able to sleep at night, and when it came time to go do some work with the Destiny Rescue crew, she was not able to go. I had to send my team and stay back with her in the heat of the day. Ashley was overwhelmed by the heat and reduced to tears, saying she wanted to go home. My plan to bring Ashley to Thailand in hopes of her falling in love with the idea of living there (and church planting there) was failing miserably.

My world was turned upside down. I knew my new wife did not love the heat, but I had no idea how badly it affected her. We realized later that for some reason she does not sweat, and since heat is not released from her body, she starts to cook.

Our good friend Nathan Densley had accompanied us on our trip. Nathan, who like me was sold on missions—especially in Southeast Asia—was feeling my pain. He knew how hard it was on me to stay back and not go out with the team. He also knew that it was not half as hard as what was going on internally for me. One of my greatest dreams, to be a missionary to Thailand one day, was not looking too promising.

After pushing through some emotions and getting creative, Ashley and I got an umbrella and some ice cold drinks to help her fight the heat. We got away to the Destiny Rescue compound one day to go spend time with the rescued children. It was so amazing to arrive and see all of the warm smiling faces excited to greet us. Our hearts melted as Ashley and I got to love on children who had been rescued from awful situations.

After hanging out at the main compound, we spent time where they kept younger kids who had been rescued along with siblings who were at risk. Some of the kids were as young as five years old. One of the workers told me that the five-year-old kids had thankfully just been taken from at-risk situations by the Thai government. And then the worker pointed to a girl who appeared to be about twelve or thirteen and told me that she had been rescued a year prior. When the Destiny Rescue team had set up the sting with the Thai police, they found the young girl chained to a bed where she was forced to have sex with clients day after day. I was so heartbroken for this precious little girl. I could not imagine what she had gone through and what she must still be going through even now after being rescued.

I was in shock at the reality of the life situations of the hundreds of kids I was spending time with in Chiang Rai, knowing they all had a very painful story and would have to journey to a place of healing and restoration that would set them up for a bright future. I was so incredibly thankful for Destiny Rescue, who not only rescued these children from a life unimaginable but also provided them with hope and healing. I was thankful for the work Destiny Rescue was doing and for every moment I got to be with them. It was amazing to witness firsthand the well-rounded work they were doing there.

Our hearts were full as we got to spend time with all of the beautiful, happy kids rescued from the sex trade. It was hard to wrap our minds around what these kids had experienced before they were rescued. I knew the Lord had brought us to Destiny Rescue and that we were there for purposes greater than ourselves. Although it was a tough time for Ashley and me, the trip was in no way a waste.

The Lord knew how difficult that time was going to be for both of us, and He supplied us with a saving grace on the last week of our trip. That grace was Deeper Still Ministries. I had made contact with Julie Smude, the founder of Deeper Still Ministries, through Keith Hazell back in Lethbridge. Julie was an amazing woman of God who had a few different ventures going on in Chiang Rai, but everything seemed to flow out of Deeper Still Ministries. Julie had a beautiful open prayer room with heavenly murals painted from end to end. The presence of God was so sweet and rested so strongly there.

If ever there would be a ministry that Ashley would want to connect with, it would be one that endeavored to go deeper. Ashley's heart for worship is always to go deeper in the spirit with the Lord. We spent a week with "Mamma Julie" (in air conditioning) praying and prophesying. The air was pregnant with expectation for what was going to take place there.

Back in Lethbridge, prior to the trip, I'd had a vision of what I can only describe as a giant pocket of glory living and breathing under the ground in Chang Rai. That vision was a defining moment for the team: we knew that we were supposed to go to Chang Rai. To this day, Thailand has never seen revival. After spending a week in intercession over Thailand, I sensed strongly that one day the earth and heaven would open up over Chang Rai and that the glory of God would be poured out like never before. Our time with Julie at Deeper Still Ministries helped to redeem the difficulty that Ashley and I had experienced due to the heat the prior week.

Although there were some difficult heart issues going on for me, it was still an amazing trip. I had made amazing new connections and got to witness Destiny Rescue's incredibly inspiring work. But as all good things come to an end, it was soon time to go back to Lethbridge and start my new career.

A month before we had left for Thailand, I had been hired at Lethbridge Family Services as a settlement counselor working with immigrants. It was a great opportunity to do what I loved, working with people from other cultures. I was both excited and terrified, as this would be my first office job. Going to school had paid off, as I now had the opportunity to do purposeful work. The only thing I would have to lift was a pen. I was still dealing with the same insecure feelings I had when I went to college, thinking I was going to fail, but thankfully I had a great manager. Bozana Sljuka, who would also become a friend, took the time to train me and welcome me to my new career.

I worked with clients who had different immigration statuses, but the majority of my time was spent helping resettle refugees. My contact with refugees started right at the airport. I would wait until a group of exhausted immigrants filed off the plane carrying their blue-and-white IOM (International Organization for Migration) bags containing all of their pertinent documents and a few large duffel bags holding all of their belongings.

The group I worked with the most was Bhutanese refugees. Many had been living in a refugee camp for the past twenty years, with only the bare minimum for provisions. The majority of them had never even turned on a shower before, so I had to give them a complete orientation on how to use the stove, washroom, and thermostat. Although it seemed like my Thailand dreams had recently been crushed, I soon forgot about it in the excitement of my new job. It was amazing to spend time with families who had literally had their lives put on hold for twenty years. They were beautiful people to be with, and it was an honor to assist them in beginning a new life in Canada. I was humbled by the experience of working with the Bhutanese, who despite the hardship of having to flee their homes and country of birth, were determined to start life again in a brand-new world—and in a brand-new language.

As I took an increasing liking to my new career, I began to wonder if I'd been wrong all those years ago not to attach myself to commitments that would prevent me from going anywhere, anytime, for the Gospel. I had now officially taken on the very roles I had scorned: I had a student loan, a mortgage, and now a career that gave me a three weeks of holidays a year—no mission trips to Thailand for me. I think what freaked me out the most was that I was OK with it. I had kingdom adventure every day at work. I was being paid a great wage to be fully engaged in social justice every day of the week. It was actually amazing.

It was a revelation that gave me the peace of mind to fully embrace the present and be released from the unbalanced expectations I had for my life. This deep, freeing revelation came once again from those red letters, the Gospels. I was reading about Jesus calling Peter to follow Him and be his disciple, and it occurred to me that Peter was busy being a fisherman. He was not sitting around waiting for Jesus to show up. I thought of every person Jesus called, and it was the same story: they all had careers and titles. Jesus called Luke, the physician, and even Mathew and Zacchaeus, who were tax collectors and who were not well loved by the people.

I was so afraid that I would miss my calling if I was committed to anything that I failed to see that I could simply commit to Jesus and allow Him to call me when He needed me. I had a poverty mentality that said I should have little so that I could be ready to do anything on a whim. I was guilty of judging Christians because of their wealth and achievements, and I had a time of repentance. I was reminded of a vision I'd had five years earlier. I had seen a picture of a perfect house on a hill with a wraparound veranda and a perfectly manicured yard hemmed in by a white picket fence. Outside of the fence was a great harvest of wheat blowing beautifully in the wind as the warm sun shone down. The energy of that vision filled me with peace and awe. It was then that the Lord said to me, "I need your heart to reflect this house. The harvest is great, and you are called to be a harvester, but first you must learn the discipline of contentment." I knew that I was to lay all things down and make Jesus the pursuit of my passion and trust, that He would make my path straight.

As I settled deeper into my roles of settlement counselor, church leader, and husband, I was about to step into another role that I had no experience with: father. Ashley was pregnant with our first son. Judah Riley Harrison arrived on October 17, 2011. With his explosive personality, Judah brought an incredible amount of joy into our home. We were so thrilled to have our little gift from God, even if he did rob us of sleep most evenings.

Life continued at a pretty steady pace over the next few years as I neared the end of my twenties. I was more stable and comfortable than ever before, and many of my "Who am I?" struggles had vanished. Every once in a while I thought back to what now seemed like wild days with Alex and Dustin on our TruthLifeDocumentary adventure. I wondered if we had been chasing a dead end or if we were really on to something. I still felt a lot of confusion about life and wounds from the past, but at least now I had some stability.

Part 3: Dreaming

10

Healing of the Heart

While sitting in my office at work one day, I received an e-mail with a familiar name in the subject line: Chad Block. Chad was an old Calgary friend of mine who had seen my employee picture on the Immigrants Services website. We got together for coffee, and it was great to reconnect. Chad had moved to Lethbridge to work with Bishop Todd Atkinson at a church called River of Life. ROL was part of a movement of churches called VIA Apostolica, which was also led by Bishop Todd. VIA focused on what they called "healing of the heart." Chad and his wife Jana had been drawn to VIA because of their own need for healing and restoration. Chad told me that one day, as he had journaled by the ocean in Comox, he had written, "I am not OK." The Lord was faithful, answering his plea for help by leading him to a place where he could work on healing and becoming whole. I was very curious to learn more.

I already had experience with counseling and deliverance, but it seemed like they were just that—experiences. I often felt disappointed and frustrated about getting healing because I needed to pay money to a counselor or wait for a person who had a deliverance ministry to come through town. It felt like the valleys and mountaintops were too long in between. I was desperate for the freedom and liberty I had been promised through the Word of God.

Ashley and I attended our first Healing of the Heart Conference at ROL, where the meetings were led by a team of charismatic Anglican ministers from Florida. I was familiar with their message from the books and material I had been reading, but it was different in a church of six hundred people who were excited to learn it together and to make healing a high priority in their lives. Teaching healing of the heart was a priority for their church calendar: the Florida team came to provide healing prayer and train teams of people in Lethbridge every year. I felt the Holy Spirit over the message and knew that the Lord was calling us deeper into our own healing journeys.

After a few long nights of prayer and conversation, both Ashley and I felt that our years of ministering alongside the Hazells at Mosaic church were coming to a close. We loved the Hazells and have continued our friendship with them, but we knew the Lord was shifting our feet. The Lord was calling us to be a part of VIA to learn and experience everything we could about healing of the heart. We knew we were supposed to walk alongside the Blocks and Bishop Todd for a season—and longer, if that's what the Lord wanted us to do. We wanted to learn more from the ministry team that came from Florida and would take every opportunity offered.

Dr. Ken Smylie and Bishop Ron Kuykendall led the team that came from Florida. I had a session with Dr. Ken, who practiced a sozo style of healing prayer (Theophostic prayer). The Greek work *sozo* means saved, whole, and healed. Sozo is an inner-healing methodology developed by ministers at Bethel Church in Redding, California. Ken's motto is: "When we rest, God works, and when we work, God rests." Ken made it clear that it was the Holy Spirit who was there to do the job and lead us in our time of prayer. Ken would simply ask what I was feeling or hearing, and I would have a negative sensation arise and tell him what it was. For example, I might hear in my spirit that I was worthless.

That was a lie that was planted in my mind by the devil. Then Ken might ask, "Where did that lie come in?" and a memory would come from my childhood—struggling in school, staying back from a field trip, or grieving that I was in trouble and not good like the other kids. I would repent of allowing that lie to take hold of me and ask that Jesus would deal with it. Then Jesus would be invited to come in and fill the space where the lie had been with his glory and life.

It was absolutely beautiful. Jesus was my counselor and healer, through Dr. Ken. There is certainly a need for traditional, conversation-based counseling, but this style of healing prayer was amazing to me. I felt light as a feather walking out of that healing session—until the next day, that is. I went from feeling like a free bird in flight to a gator wallowing through the mud. It was a familiar feeling to me, one I recognized from the aftermath of deliverance prayer. It was so confusing. I knew the Lord was in everything that was happening, yet I felt like hell the next day.

I was working out in the gym on my lunch break a day or two later when I ran into the muscleman himself, Bishop Todd. Todd asked me how I had enjoyed the conference and my time with Dr. Ken. I told him that my time was great, but I had been feeling like crap ever since. Todd smiled, as if he understood exactly what I was saying, then told me that he had gone through the same thing. The Lord showed him the parable of Jesus healing the blind man by spitting in the mud and rubbing it in his eyes. He said that Jesus had told him it would get a whole lot muddier before it got clear. Having our hearts open and exposed puts us in a vulnerable state. I needed to learn how to manage myself better as I came out of such intense memories.

I also needed to manage myself as I went into healing times. Before each Healing of the Heart Conference, there were always a number of people who wondered if they were losing it. The Lord allows us to feel some depth to the pain that rests in our souls so we are aware that it's there in order to address it and get it out. It can be especially scary for people who are new to a culture of healing and do not know what it looks like to come out on the other side. I felt relieved that I was not the only one who went through pain and confusing moments during healing. I positioned myself differently with prayer before and after healing from then on. I was building a new depth to my foundation, and I was hungry for more.

Ashley and I prayed and felt that the Lord was leading us to go to Florida to spend a week at the "Car Wash," as the healing team led by Dr. Ken had nicknamed their ministry. The Lord provided finances for us by having friends and family offer us money, which brought a special confirmation to our hearts that we should invest our time and finances with Dr. Ken's team, seeking healing that would improve our lives and our marriage, and help us build a healthy family. We set a date to fly to Florida and completed a questionnaire package to be filled out before we arrived. The package included a wide range of questions addressing substance abuse, witchcraft, sexual relationships, and child abuse. Ashley and I filled out the eight-page questionnaire, sent it off, and then followed our letters to Florida.

Dr. Ken had two homes side by side in the "Turkey Forest." Our little place had all we needed. We had no television or Internet and were forced to do nothing but rest, talk, read, journal, and pray. Of the two of us, I think Ashley was more intimidated by the lack of distractions.

The next morning we went into our first session. Dr. Ken wanted to give us some direction about what the week would look like and to talk about some of our answers to the questionnaire. Due to my colorful past, my questionnaire was a lot more marked up than Ashley's, and there was one particular item on the list that I wanted to talk to Ken about before we got going.

When I was a child, a male babysitter had sexually abused my siblings and me. I told Ken that I had received counseling for this in the past and so I did not feel like I needed to give it much attention. I thought I had already dealt with it. When I gave my life to the Lord, I was aware that I needed to forgive everyone in my life in order to be forgiven, and I remember praying and confessing my forgiveness toward the abuser. The reason I wanted Ken to know more about my abuse was that although I had forgiven the abuser, I had recently become aware of anger rising up toward the church and my family for failing to protect me. I was also having some flashbacks of the aftermath, when the abuser was exposed.

I remembered walking down Pettegrew Road toward home when my dad's best friend, who we called Uncle Dave, pulled over and told me that I needed to come back with him to my parents' house. I thought to myself, "Oh no, what am I getting in trouble for now?" I came home to find the abuser and his family there, ready to have a meeting with my family. I don't remember the meeting itself, but I have talked about it with my brother—who was eight at the time—as we discussed coping with a pain that never went away.

I have three distinct memories of the abuse. In addition to going home for the meeting, I recall making a deal with the abuser to do what he asked if he would let me go to the air show with our friend down the street and then walking from my house to the neighbor's with a great deal of shame after the terms of the deal were met. And lastly, I remember seeing him at school. He remained a student at our tiny little Christian school even after he had been caught in the abuse. I remember being outside for recess as a six-year-old child, fully cognizant that he should not be there. I was angry and wanted to hurt him. Although I had forgiven the abuser, the pain of the experience was still alive. It was repressed, but it was very much alive.

After doing a healing session with Ken, I received revelation of the ripple effect of the pain and confusion stemming from the abuse. It was finally starting to make some sense. I had been six years old, just beginning a very important time in my intellectual development and education. For the first time, I understood that I had not been a dumb kid but a traumatized one. My short attention span was due to numbness and to an imagination that wanted to escape every facet of reality. As I took a deep breath of relief—connecting to the pain of a new level of understanding of my past—I also became more aware of the anger and sadness directed toward my parents because they had missed the signs and did not identify the trauma I was experiencing.

That trauma had affected me not only emotionally but physically. I was sick a lot as a kid and was taken to doctor after doctor to see what was wrong with me. I suffered a lot of stomachaches. After multiple tests, I was sent to a specialist who went so far as to perform a small surgery on me, getting inside to see if he could find something wrong. Unfortunately, trauma does not show up in a physical examination. My nervous system was a wreck. I ended up developing ulcers and vomiting blood and frequently finding it in my stool.

When I think back to the abuse from my babysitter, the sadness does not even come near to the memory of a little boy who was spanked time and time again because he could not focus at school and did whatever it took to get through a day, even if it meant cheating. The sexual abuse was traumatic, but the school abuse and naive-fueled neglect added up to another nine years of trauma.

When we pursue healing, we need to be clear that we are not selling people out or trying to point a finger at those who have hurt us. Much of the time, those people don't even need to know that they have caused pain. People hurt one another often: it's the human condition. I, for one, have likely hurt more people than the average person. Because my mom and dad are my biggest cheerleaders in my healing process, I have been blessed by their love and willingness to communicate and revisit hard times, and I am able to work it out with them. Remember, it was my parents who put me with the abuser, and my dad was the head of the school that traumatized me. As we dive into the past and painful memories are exposed, there can be many layers to the pain. It is important to get to the root experiences that have a stronghold and deal with them. After these roots have been dealt with, we follow the "pain trail" and clean out every bad memory and experience that was connected to it so we can heal.

The healing of the heart journey is not an easy one. Bishop Todd was right: my healing journey did get a lot muddier before things got clear. Having to go back and face my fears as I dug up those painful memories was no easy task, but it was necessary.

The Lord did a lot for Ashley and me in Gainesville that week, but by far the greatest gift was my new knowledge of the events that had triggered my self-concept as dumb and worthless. Working with Dr. Ken was such a blessing because he let the Holy Spirit do His part in revealing where the pain was. Then Ken was able to use his education about the effects of trauma to create a well-rounded picture of understanding for me. It was a great relief to have some understanding of the deep, dark hole in my heart. When we understand where our pain comes from, we can see its effect on our lives. We can also be sure then that God is true to his word: Jesus comes to redeem everything that the father of lies has stolen.

11

The 400 Pound Male Stripper

I first met Derrick Shirley when my manager at Lethbridge Family Services sent me to a training seminar he was hosting. All I knew was that Derrick had an education in psychology and had recently written a book. I went to a lot of training seminars for work, and they were usually snoozers, but Derrick had me captivated almost immediately. There was a weight to his words as he told us his story.

Derrick's book was called *The 400 Pound Male Stripper*. In it, Derrick described his upbringing as one enveloped in confusion. He was half white and half black, living in a predominantly white neighborhood. Constantly heckled with racist comments, he decided one day that he'd had enough of being black and would only embrace his white side from then on. He made light of his struggle as he told us about how he grew a mullet and spent school dances pretending that he could not dance well in order to fit in with the rest of the white kids.

Derrick said that his broken identity took him down a dark road. He himself became racist and shared painful memories as he began to lash out against other black men. After Derrick finished school, he found himself a broken man working as a bouncer in strip bars. Once a slender and handsome man, he became an emotional eater and was transformed into a four-hundred-pound couch potato. He knew he was slowly dying and needed to make some major life changes.

Eventually, Derrick found healing through pen and paper and is now able to trace his pain back to those internal decisions made in childhood. Pain caused him to change himself by picking up a "script" that he thought would gain him acceptance. In *The 400 Hounded Pound Male Stripper*, he explains how we are all given a script to follow from birth. Derrick writes:

> When an actor assumes a role in a play or a movie, they are given a script. When a classical musician is asked to play a piece, they are given a musical score. When a framer is asked to construct a house they are given a blue print. There is room for some variation in how the role is played, how long the note is held, or how fast the house is built, but to be a successful actor, musician, or framer it is expected that one follow the script of the guidelines and the plan. In many ways we are not unlike an actor playing a role. The second we are born we are labeled and a script is given to us. Our first label was "boy" or "girl." The familiar script that follows says boys wear blue and girls wear pink; boys play with cars and girls play with dolls. Boys play sports and girls join dance; boys get angry and girls cry (Shirley 2012).

When people shut down part of who they truly are, it creates a black hole of emptiness. Derrick said the greatest healing for him came from becoming self-aware of his scripts and then writing about them as therapy. Derrick did not stop at getting healing for his mind and emotions: he radically changed his physical life. He went from a sedentary four-hundred-pound man to a triathlon athlete with a six-pack. Derrick ran across Canada, not only to face his demons, but in hopes of writing a story that would inspire all who heard it. Derrick's story gives its audience the courage to dig deep and ask what scripts they have picked up.

As I had been in counseling a number of years working out my own pain and depression, much of his story was familiar to me. I had long ago acknowledged and dropped my life's most damaging script, the one that convinced me I was stupid. I was cheering Derrick on as he spoke, able to identify with him in deep places, and yet there was a nagging ache I could feel growing in my heart. Derrick was talking not only about rewriting fragments of our stories but about getting us to look at our whole story. What were we doing with our lives? What was our dream job? What stamp did we want to leave on the earth in our day? Once again, I wondered: *Who am I?*

For the three years following the trip Ashley and I had taken to Thailand, I had continued to work at Immigrant Services. Although I felt settled for the first time in my life, I became aware that day that I was not completely OK with staying where I was. Here was an educated man, successfully speaking on the message that had driven me throughout my twenties. It's not that I did not like my job, but I had to ask myself, "When did I quit dreaming?" The part of me that was a dreamer had settled, and I had a conviction to revisit my dreams. I got vulnerable with my journal that evening and wrote, "What would I like to do with my life?"

The following is my journal entry from January 26, 2013:

> What do I want to do?
> Who do I want to be?
> Who do I want to be something for?
> What will my story be?
> I want my great grandchildren and my great, great, grandchildren to remember my name. I want to leave something of a special inheritance for my family. I want to do well in all respects.
> So what then?

So what then is my calling? To know my calling, to know my burden and master it. Ultimately to see people released into their callings. To see the worth, to see the obstacles, and to see the end result. I feel my calling is both national and international. Those who I see living in physical, emotional, and spiritual slavery at the hand of injustice are the faces that bring me a brokenness that I cannot hide. In the countries where the Good News has not shaped government, those fatherless nations, I want to be a master builder, positioning brick and mortar—people and gifts—in places of potential and influence. Seeing the kingdom built all over the earth.

I want to have influence. I want maximum knowledge in expertise of identity, healing, and counseling. I want to be more than financially stable but flexible. I want to have my foot in the professional world and the church. I want to be the master of my schedule, recognizing that how much I would give to others would be costly so my family would not take a back seat to my calling. My wife's calling and my children's callings would joyfully be my number-one priority, yet I know unless I engage in my own calling 100 percent they would never fully engage in their own 100 percent. I must submit to the grace of my calling, and all will fall in place as I step out...

As I dug deep into the most tender parts of my heart, there was Thailand; it had not gone anywhere. I saw those rescued Thai children's faces smiling back at me, and I remembered those in the brothels who had not been rescued. I thought about the past ten years of my life, my twenties, and how they had been a time of self-discovery and healing. That evening I journaled about the power of healing and identity reformation. I put value on continuing my personal healing journey, as I knew I had a ways to go. The question rose in my mind, "What do I have to offer Thailand, and the world around me?" That night, a new dream was born. I decided I wanted to go back to school and become a therapeutic counselor.

What better thing could I do than to share the gift of healing and help guide those precious ones back to themselves? Maybe—just maybe—I could share my story of healing and inspire others, like Derrick inspired me, to go back to the vulnerable and often painful question, "Who am I?" It takes great bravery to stare age-old pain in the eye, expose it, and then deny it any more access to your life. It takes time to completely forget the scripts you've picked up and walk in the truth of who you are, but it can be done. I was ready to expose my heart to dreaming again.

About the time Ashley and I had made the difficult decision to leave Mosaic Christian Fellowship to pursue training in Healing of the Heart, I received an e-mail from Julie Smude of Deeper Still Ministries in Chiang Rai. She sent me a one-line message that read, "The oak is in the acorn." I hadn't had any contact with Julie, other than the odd Facebook "Like" since we had left Chiang Rai three years earlier. What was this prophetic riddle? Ashley and I were astounded by the timing yet perplexed by its meaning.

Little did we know that not only were we starting out in a new church, we were about to start life in a new place. Chad and Janna were only going to be in Lethbridge for a few more months, as they were getting ready to move back to the Comox Valley on Vancouver Island to plant a church. As Ashley and I connected more with Chad and Janna, we felt that the Lord was calling us to uproot and be a part of the team that was going to plant the church. I knew that I wanted to go back to school for psychology and counseling, but we had no idea how we could make it work financially. I was quickly understanding the meaning of the acorn. It was an exciting new beginning but a vulnerable one. All that was familiar to our little family was in Lethbridge.

Our little family of three was also about to grow by one: Ashley was pregnant with our second child. We had just begun to establish ourselves financially and had the invaluable support of Ashley's parents, who often provided childcare for our son, Judah. I was sure I had heard the Lord say that we were to go to Comox, and it made no financial sense to start a new journey of education there, but I was sure that is what this little acorn had heard. As I sat at home in my study every night reading my Bible and praying, I fought anxiety about whether we could make it there or not. Every evening I had an old worship song from the nineties playing in mind, "He will make a way, where there seems to be no way. / He works in ways we cannot see: He will make a way for me. / He will make a way."

We were supposed to be moving to Comox in a matter of months, but our finances had taken a hit because our house needed some repairs and we needed to buy a vehicle. One evening Ashley and I had gone to A&W for supper, and when I went to pay for our food my debit card had insufficient funds. I was worried, wondering how in the world we could be planning to move when we could not afford A&W.

I decided the only option was to take control of the situation by selling our houses, which ended up being a whole lot of wasted time and energy. We had purchased a second home in Lethbridge a few years earlier and were renting out our first home. When I initially worked it out on paper, I thought it would be best for us to rent out both of our Lethbridge homes and rent a home in Comox. I started to wonder whether or not it would be too difficult to have houses rented out in Lethbridge while living in Comox and decided to make an attempt to sell them. Selling homes is a very emotional process. We ended up selling our rental home twice, and it fell through both times. I was absolutely gutted and did not understand why God was not pushing the house sale through. I got quite disillusioned and then remembered how I'd initially thought the best plan was to rent them out. I decided to trust the Lord to provide faithful renters.

I was at my wit's end trying to make things happen myself. Although I thought the only possible way we could afford to move to Comox and go to school was to sell our house, the Lord had other plans. I was to rest and trust in Him. Bishop Joseph Garlington says, "God opens one door and closes another, but it's hell in the hallway." It is truly hard in the in between, but that is usually because of our own doubts and negative thoughts. I was struggling at times with thoughts like, "I know God does these kind of provision-type miracles for others, but will He do it for me?" It became so much easier as I laid everything down and said, "You are good, and only good, and I trust you to provide if that is where you are calling us."

Ashley was such a rock for me in that time. She stood firm, believing that if the Lord was already stretching us to move away from our support system with no jobs and a baby on the way, He would provide. I was finally beginning to believe the words of the song I had been meditating on for months: He would make a way. And once I started to believe, one by one, doors started opening.

A bunch of small miracles added up to one big miracle. The biggest miracle was that I had unknowingly started a savings account. I had been filing my taxes wrong for five years and was supposed to be claiming all of the interest on the mortgage of my rental home. The government owed us several thousand dollars. Before we found out about the income tax money we were going to receive, there was a point when Ashley and I decided, even when we had no money to move, that we were going "all in." Even though it looked like we had no money to move, we knew God was calling us to Comox. And since He was calling us, He would provide in a way we could not see at that time. The money we needed to move arrived to us one week after we arrived in Comox.

On March 15, 2014, we packed up all of our belongings and moved to Comox Valley to join the church plant called VIA Comox. Our son, Rowan Davey Harrison, was born to us in Comox on April 29, 2014, and he was perfect. The Lord blessed us financially beyond our expectations, and as I started to write this book in January of 2015, I had also begun full-time studies in psychology and counseling. I am the most blessed acorn in the world. I have been able to rest under the shadow of the Almighty God and to be amazed as He shows me His love and faithfulness. My heart, mind, and emotions have received such healing these past years, as I have been learning what it means to be a son to the One who is love. I still have a ways to go to become an oak, but I can say that I am truly enjoying the journey. The destination will come when it comes.

12

God's Dream

One evening, driving home with my wife and son from my in-laws' cabin near Fernie, British Columbia, I had an awesome experience—in the full extent of the word. Ashley and Judah were both asleep in the car, and I felt so close to God and the Kingdom of Heaven that night that I wondered if I was going to die. I was white-knuckling the steering wheel, just waiting for a moose or a semi to jump out at me.

In that moment, I heard the Lord speak, perhaps more clearly than I had ever heard Him speak to me before. I heard Him say, "I love you." I dared to ask if He would speak to me again, and He did. He said, "I will never leave you nor forsake you." I then had a flash of a very random memory pass through my mind. I could see myself at around the age of ten, walking through the hallway of the Estevan Hospital as a candy striper. As I saw myself walking in that memory, I could sense the presence of God strong with that ten-year-old child. I asked Him again, "Lord will you speak to me one more time?" And He said, "I have plans for you, a future to prosper you."

I did not ask any more questions, and we did not meet a moose or a semi. It was simply a divine moment where I heard the voice of the Lord so clearly and it shook me to my core. I was truly overcome by the clarity of His voice and His promises to me that evening.

Jeremiah 29:11 (NIV) states: "For I know the plans I have for you, declares the Lord, plans to prosper you and not to harm you, plans to give you hope and a future". Wow, what a promise! How important it is to believe that the Lord has a plan for our lives. It is critical that we never lose hope in our calling.

We are God's dream. The Lord has a plan to give us a future and a hope. When we connect with our dreams, we are connecting with God's plan for our lives. I believe that as I dream I can lay my life down to the Lord, and He will 100 percent guide my steps. If you believe the Word of God, then you can trust Him to take you to the destination—as long as you're willing to do your part and accept His timing.

I remember Pastor Jeremy, in Lethbridge, talking to me about surfing. He said, "We all love riding a great wave, but the majority of our lives are not spent riding waves but paddling." For me, much of the "wilderness" I've gone through has been a test of my patience. The Lord has done a tremendous amount in my life in every season, but I have not yet arrived. I have not arrived at the destination of my dream, nor have I arrived with the character to carry the responsibility of my dream.

It can be hard to hear the age-old saying, "It's not the destination but the journey." I think most people who quote that old proverb are people who have a completed journey to look back on. For many people, it can be agonizing to see the dream of the Lord appearing just out of their reach. It may be a true saying, but that does not make it easy to hear.

When I look back over the past several years, I recognize that I have been in training. The Lord and I are in a game of chess, but we are on the same team. He leads me into every move. Because I barely know how to play chess, I am extremely dependent on Him. I may think I understand the game of life, but in fact, I don't. As the Lord leads us, He sets us up for the best result. Patience is key between moves. Jeremy also used to say that we are not sprint runners, we are training for a marathon. I think a very long relay race might also be a good metaphor. We are not just running for ourselves: the baton will keep moving well after we're gone if we do it God's way. I need constant reminders that I am in training and am setting up a foundation for my life and dreams.

If I'm not careful, I can begin to feel that God is cruel, that He allows these dreams and gives us His green light, but that they will never come true. Or even more strongly, I may feel that I will never be good enough to follow through with the dreams of my heart. There have been times when my dreams felt unattainable. I have thought at times that God might not choose to use me after all, a feeling rooted in low self-esteem and low self-worth. The truth is that the Lord thinks I am an all-star. The Lord is training me, and He is not in a hurry. At times like these, I need to retreat into places of creativity and disciplines that refuel me and refocus my eyes on the goal. Eventually, my heart fills with the spirit of patient endurance, and I am OK.

As we dream about what the best calling for us might look like, we often do so from a perspective of reflecting on and evaluating the callings of other people. We see the preacher whose charisma rallies the people into action, the businessperson who is raising millions to combat poverty, or the anointed worship leader who tours the world. The people we look up to influence the direction we want to take in life. It's OK to desire to be fruitful like our heroes, but we have to recognize that God made us unique and that He has a calling set apart for us that may resemble many other people's callings. And we must remember that our calling will always be authentic to us. Bill Johnson says, "When you find out what God has made you for, you do not want to be anyone else." This is revival: when the people of God choose to live out the royal call of heaven over their lives on earth.

And then there are those who have a sense of what God wants them to do in this life, but the dream looks too big and too scary—*how on earth could little old me do that*? Insecurity and low self-esteem are dream-killers. Far too many believers have a low perception of themselves. They say, "Even if I believed that I could walk out this dream, no one else would believe in me." Thankfully, God does not view us as we view ourselves, from the lens of our brokenness. God's prophet Samuel was supposed to find God's new chosen king to annoint after King Saul had disobeyed God and was no longer called to be king. To Samuel's surprise the next person God called was the youngest and most unlikely of all his brothers, David. As 1 Samuel 16:7 (NIV) says, "But the Lord said to Samuel, 'Do not consider his appearance or his height, for I have rejected him. The Lord does not look at the things people look at. People look at the outward appearance, but the Lord looks at the heart," Some people receive the dream of God and think that it would be better passed off to the next guy—he has all the looks and talent, after all.

The people of God need to be healed and believe. The Lord did not write "REJECT" into anyone's DNA code. We are *all*, in the words of Psalm 139 (NIV), "fearfully and wonderfully made." God made us perfect for the life He has for us. Can you imagine what the church would look like—what the world would look like—if we all accepted that, if we all loved ourselves and boldly stepped into God's dream for our lives?

There is a great tension in the pursuit of dreams. I once believed I should have nothing, do nothing, and always be ready to go to the nations. Then things shifted as the Lord led me into a much different lifestyle: college, career, house, and family.

Believers must strike a balance between moving forward in our calling, fighting the battle that He has called us to fight, and feeling the freedom to move forward with life when God does not seem to be speaking. Where does free will fit in? There are long seasons for many during which they do not feel His leadership and are faced with too many choices: "Should I go to school? Should I go to YWAM? Should I work and help out with the youth group?" How do we move forward without worrying about fighting the wrong battles or making the wrong decisions?

When I was a kid, my little sister had a Tamagotchi. If you know what I am talking about, you remember the nineties. Tamagotchis were little digital animals on a keychain. One day, as I was sitting in church listening to my good friend Will preach on his relationship with God, I got to thinking about Tamagotchis in relation to our free will. Tamagotchis were these generally useless toys that you had to feed and put to sleep, or they would beep at you. They were the most unentertaining pets you could ever imagine. The only entertainment I ever got from my sister's toy was when I would hide it and watch her frantically search the house so it would not starve itself—sorry, Kaylah!

We are not God's pets, and He has given us more brains than a keychain computer. We are God's children. I have seen some Christians who fear decision making because they are afraid they will do the wrong thing and disappoint God somehow, and this is not the way He wants us to feel. God has empowered us. He loves seeing us step out and be ourselves. He has never desired to control us. If He wanted to do so, he would have put the tree of the Knowledge of Good and Evil in a place where Adam and Eve could never get to it. We are to live out of a loving relationship with the Lord, in tandem with him. He wants to see us step out, take risks, and grow into our potential. He wants us to be authentic.

I believe that some people are afraid to dream and to pursue dreams because they are afraid they will deviate from God's plans. What I am trying to get at is that God put a dream in each of us at birth. The very DNA that he wove into our beings set a path for us to follow. The Bible says, "Man makes plans in his heart, and the Lord orders his steps" (Proverbs 16:9 (NIV).

So if I am not a Tamagotchi and the Lord has given me freedom to pursue a career, how can I know I am making the right decision? I want to step out, but I want to follow God's will for my life—and I really want to be sure. This is a question I have often asked along the way, and I believe it is a common one. When I am working out my ideas and plans, I pray a simple prayer. I pray for the Lord to open doors and close them according to His will and with every decision I make. As I feel I am bound by His grace in the first place, this prayer seems to work 100 percent of the time.

There are seasons where the Lord gives us very clear direction. He may tell us to go to Africa and start an orphanage or to go to university for engineering. There are also seasons where we ask for direction and it does not seem to come. So what do we do when we seem to have no direction? Do we wait and do nothing? No, this is a time to make plans in our heart. There is a maturity that comes with understanding that God put some really good stuff into us at birth. We need to discipline our hearts and minds to believe it.

Psalm 139 beautifully displays truth and promise about who we are and our connection to our Creator. It paints a picture of how God intimately involves Himself in our lives. It is from this passage that I have such confidence that the God of love cares not only for me but in the small and great details of my life, that He knew me before birth and will watch and guide me until my dying day.

Psalm 139
For the director of music. Of David. A psalm.

1
You have searched me, Lord,
    and you know me.
2
You know when I sit and when I rise;
    you perceive my thoughts from afar.

3
You discern my going out and my lying down;
    you are familiar with all my ways.

4
Before a word is on my tongue
    you, Lord, know it completely.

5
You hem me in behind and before,
    and you lay your hand upon me.

6
Such knowledge is too wonderful for me,
    too lofty for me to attain.

7
Where can I go from your Spirit?
    Where can I flee from your presence?

8
If I go up to the heavens, you are there;
    if I make my bed in the depths, you are there.

9
If I rise on the wings of the dawn,
    if I settle on the far side of the sea,

10
even there your hand will guide me,
    your right hand will hold me fast.

11
If I say, "Surely the darkness will hide me
    and the light become night around me,"

12
even the darkness will not be dark to you;
    the night will shine like the day,
    for darkness is as light to you.

13
For you created my inmost being;
    you knit me together in my mother's womb.

14

I praise you because I am fearfully and wonderfully made;
    your works are wonderful,
    I know that full well.

15

My frame was not hidden from you
    when I was made in the secret place,
    when I was woven together in the depths of the earth.

16

Your eyes saw my unformed body;
    all the days ordained for me were written in your book
    before one of them came to be.

17

How precious to me are your thoughts, God!
    How vast is the sum of them!

18

Were I to count them,
    they would outnumber the grains of sand—
    when I awake, I am still with you.

19

If only you, God, would slay the wicked!
    Away from me, you who are bloodthirsty!

20

They speak of you with evil intent;
    your adversaries misuse your name.

21

Do I not hate those who hate you, Lord,
    and abhor those who are in rebellion against you?

22

I have nothing but hatred for them;
    I count them my enemies.

23

Search me, God, and know my heart;
    test me and know my anxious thoughts.

24

See if there is any offensive way in me,
    and lead me in the way everlasting.

Psalm 139 says that God has knit each of us together in our mother's womb: how can I not be confident that He has a plan for my life? I think back to when I struggled in construction, when I felt I was unemployable, when I thought I was a stupid failure. I remember when I wanted so badly to be a missionary to Asia but realized that God was not then calling me there and I could not go without His lead. I felt so hopeless that I wished the earth would just swallow me up. The Lord had to arrange a complete paradigm shift in my thinking. My perception of myself did not match the freedom and calling that the Lord had laid out for me at birth. The freedom came when I heard these sweet words: He loves me. He will never leave me, nor forsake me. He has a plan and a future for me.

13

I Am

I want to share the story of a man who has become one of my heroes. Billy Mills's story is a great inspiration to me. Billy Mills, also known as *Makata Taka Hela*, was born June 30, 1938, in Pine Ridge, South Dakota, and raised on the impoverished Pine Ridge Indian Reservation for Oglala Sioux. He was orphaned when he was twelve years old and was sent to a boarding school in Lawrence, Kansas. The racial prejudice he encountered during his time in Kansas almost drove him to suicide. As Billy writes, "There was a point where I was standing on a chair in front of an open window, about to jump, but everything under my skin said 'Don't. Don't.' It was then that I got down and wrote on a sheet of paper: 'Gold medal, 1964. Believe. Believe. Believe. Believe.'" Billy was one of the lucky ones. Instead of turning to drugs and self-harm, he used running as his coping mechanism.

Billy went on to demolish all records at his school and qualified for the Olympics. Despite the odds, Billy rose above the hand he was dealt and went on to win a gold medal in the ten thousand meter 1964 Tokyo Olympics, becoming the only person from the Western hemisphere to win the Olympic gold in this event.

In the last leg of the race, Billy said he could not hear anything except for his heart pounding. Then, although he was in third place, he could hear himself saying, "I won! I won!" just as he had visualized so many times while training for the Olympics.

He then defied all the odds as he passed the two men who stood in the way of his dream. A vision is key to successfully reaching our goals. We need to see—and believe in—the success of whatever it is we're working for.

In the years after the Olympics, Billy Mills went on to be a humanitarian and a motivational speaker. It was said that Billy gave himself to so many charities that he traveled three hundred days out of the year. Billy Mills is definitely one of my heroes. His life inspires me, and his message lives on in my heart. Billy's public speaking, as he shared his life with people all over the world, is responsible for some of my favorite quotes. Here are a few:

> *"I don't want to just tell people about my dream. I want them to take that journey to the center of their soul, and then start to solidify their dreams and find it."*
>
> *"Every dream has its passion, and every passion has its destiny."*
>
> *"If you tell people your dream, and nobody is laughing at it...then you're not dreaming big enough."*
>
> *"The greatest challenge for all of us is in what I call perceptions. We have to do all we can to change those perceptions."*

The last quote, in particular, could not be more true. Billy could have seen himself as an abandoned kid with no purpose, no reason, and no motivation to go on, but he made a decision to live. As we find our hearts on the dreaming journey, we need to make bold statements about who we are and what we're going to do. As Billy wrote, "Believe! Believe! Believe!" We need to do the same: regardless of our own situations, we need to write *believe*. We need to believe that God has a dream for us. He has a plan, a hope, and a future for our lives.

As I have written this book, my dream has grown. Originally, I had a dream of raising $15,000 with the sales of my book for the war against the sex trade—which is the cost of rescuing one child, who is then brought through all the processes that will set him or her up for a new beginning and a future. My hope was to rescue and restore at least one of the precious children who have been robbed of their innocence. I then realized that people might not laugh or shrug at that, so in the words of Billy Mills, I was dreaming too small. I now have a dream to raise a million dollars with my book—and to inspire others to dream of creative ways that they too can give themselves to projects that raise awareness and finances for social justice issues.

When I said to myself that I wanted to raise $15,000, I was setting a goal. There is a difference between setting goals and dreaming. When we set goals, we measure the distance of the goal based on our own ability and based off the measure of our self-worth. When we dream, there is a conscious decision to look past our own perception of ourselves and look full of hope toward a goal that is beyond our own ability.

When we dream, we spend time visualizing, achieving the unachievable. When we see ourselves crossing the finish line like Billy Mills, it actually changes our perception of our ability to fulfill the dream. Visualization also helps us to face the critics. If you are a dreamer, you will always have critics. In most cases, the dreamer is his own biggest critic, but you will always find people who want to give you well-meaning advice to be "realistic." Realistic people set goals; dreamers achieve the impossible.

I know that in my case, when I am in the initial stage of a dream, I have to be very careful with it. I become pregnant with the vision and carry it like a mother carries her baby, a newborn not yet ready to face the world of onlookers. Gradually, like a parent with a new baby, I have my closest friends and family come in and witness my vision. Finally, once the dream has some momentum, it is time to release it out into the vulnerable world of opinion. At this point, my love and passion for the dream is enough to celebrate it with the world of supporters and critics.

I want to inspire people to ask themselves if they truly know who they are and what their dreams are. Dreaming is the key to destiny, and a God-given destiny is much greater than the person who holds it—it can affect entire nations. I believe there are many people out there, like me, who will meet their own "Sunny" and be wrecked with compassion that gets such a tight hold on them that they are dying to help. Part of the process when a dream is released is exposure to a world greater than oneself, a world with great needs. The world needs champions who will rise up, take a risk, and stand in the face of injustice.

Remember my friend Angel, in Thailand, and our story of God revealing himself to the people of her home village? Well, Angel was faced with the decision to take a risk and make some sacrifices to remain in that place as a world-changer. Angel's faith was so encouraged after our team shared the Gospel in her home village that she continued to pray for God to send more Christians her way. She prayed for people to disciple new believers in the ways of Christ and prevent the youth there from going out to the cities to be prostituted. As she prayed for them, compassion filled her heart, and she began to dream of how she could make an impact for the kingdom.

After much time, prayer, and dreaming, Angel moved back to her home village and both began a well-received outreach program for youth and also established J Farms, an organic agricultural venture that feeds the girls rescued from the sex trade as well as volunteers for the outreach effort. Angel had to make a big sacrifice in leaving Pattaya, as she had become a accustomed to the life of a city girl, but her compassionate heart for her people could not be denied. She answered the call.

It is people like Angel and Tony Kirwan, who allow their exposure to social injustice to influence their dreams, who become world-changers. They are heroes. One thing they would both tell you, however, is that they are very normal people. As Tony has said, he is just an ordinary man with a God-sized dream.

When we fail to expose ourselves to the needs of our world and to the needs of our neighbors, we deny the world a very important answer to its pain. Oridnary people like you and I are called to make the difference. When we fail to dream and take action, the injustice of our world advances unchallanged.

The writer and theologian G. K. Chesterton was once asked to write an essay on what was wrong with the contemporary world. His reply? "Dear sirs, I am. Signed, G. K. Chesterton."

The healing of our world will not come from the answer for poverty or the cure for cancer. Heaven on earth, rather, looks like the sons and daughters of God dreaming and walking in the fullness of their calling. The world needs change, and you and I are the world-changers. We are called to feel, to dream, and to action. When we let the wounds of our neighbor affect our hearts, we answer that call. Your dreams hold the key to someone's freedom.

Afterward: The Million-Dollar Question

Play along with me: you just won a million dollars in the lottery—a lottery with a stipulation. All of the money has to be donated to a charity of your choice. Take a minute, but don't think too long. Decide where the money will go. Got it? Now write it down.

If, as you read this book, you have been reflecting on a destiny greater than yourself and wondering where to give your heart, you may have just gotten your answer. Mathew 6:21 says, "Wherever your treasure is, there your heart will be also"(NIV). Let that sink in for a minute.

You may have thought about giving money to orphanages or using the money for microloans in impoverished areas. Maybe you thought of an amazing drop-in center for your community. The million dollar question is, where is your heart?

The answer to that question, for me, began with the healing and restoration of my true identity. As we get healing for our lives and come into our true selves, we can dream from a reality that was not once available to us. I want to leave you with the following questions. Will you take the healing journey? Will you lay down the negative scripts you picked up? Will you expose yourself to a world greater than yourself and let the pain of it plant a God-sized dream in your heart? Will you change the world?

I am David Harrison, son of the Most High. I am a world-changer. I am a father to the fatherless. I dream of making an impact on the sex trade in my lifetime. I dream of seeing the restoration of people's souls. I dream of inspiring men and women to take their lives seriously and dream with God. I believe that I am the answer for a broken world.

Who are you?

Notes

About The Author

David Harrison holds one diploma in criminal justice and another in counseling and psychology.

He worked as a settlement practitioner in Lethbridge, Alberta, assisting refugees as they settled into new lives in Canada. He left this career to continue his education and begin his own business as a motivational speaker and counselor—inspired by work that has taken him across North America, Africa, Europe, and Asia.

Active in church leadership for eight years, Harrison participates in the planting of new churches in communities needing spiritual guidance. He is currently studying with the intention of becoming a registered counselor in Canada.

He currently resides in Lethbridge, AB, Canada, with his wife, Ashley, and two sons, Judah and Rowan.

To follow David's future projects or to get in contact with him for speaking engagements visit www.davidharrison.co or email info@davidharrison.co

References

Destiny Rescue
PO Box 752
North Webster, Indiana 46555
usa@destinyrescue.org
Destiny Rescue USA, Inc. is a (501)(c)(3) organization.

Derrick Shirley, *The 400 Pound Male Stripper*
Copyright 2012, Published by Zana Books

New International Version. [Colorado Springs]: Biblica, 2011. BibleGateway.com. Web. 3 Nov. 2015.

Running Strong for American Indian Youth® 2014 a 501(c)(3) organization. http://indianyouth.org/billy-mills Web. 3 Nov. 2015.

Norman Grubb, Rees Howels Intercessor
Copyright 1952, Published by Lutterworth Press

American Chesterton Society
https://www.chesterton.org/wrong-with-world/ Web 3. Nov. 2015